PYTHON
FOR
ABSOLUTE BEGINNERS

LICENSE, DISCLAIMER OF LIABILITY, AND LIMITED WARRANTY

PYTHON
FOR
ABSOLUTE BEGINNERS

Oswald Campesato

MERCURY LEARNING AND INFORMATION
Boston, Massachusetts

Publisher: David Pallai
MERCURY LEARNING AND INFORMATION
121 High Street, 3rd Floor
Boston, MA 02210
info@merclearning.com
www.merclearning.com
800-232-0223

O. Campesato. *Python for Absolute Beginners.*
ISBN: 978-1-50152-198-0

Library of Congress Control Number: 2023945505
232425321   Printed on acid-free paper in the United States of America.

Our titles are available for adoption, license, or bulk purchase by institutions, corporations, etc. For additional information, please contact the Customer Service Dept. at 800-232-0223(toll free).

All of our titles are available in digital format at *academiccourseware.com* and other digital vendors. *Companion files are available for download by writing to the publisher at info@merclearning.com.* The sole obligation of MERCURY LEARNING AND INFORMATION to the purchaser is to replace the book, based on defective materials or faulty workmanship, but not based on the operation or functionality of the product.

*I'd like to dedicate this book to my parents
– may this bring joy and happiness into their lives.*

CONTENTS

PREFACE

WHAT IS THE PRIMARY VALUE PROPOSITION FOR THIS BOOK?

This book eases you into the foundational aspects of Python 3.x with an extensive range of code samples that illustrate its diverse features. Start with Python tools and installations, and progressively learn intricacies like strings, loops, conditional logic, and much more. The appendix on NumPy provides insights into efficient numerical operations, making it a holistic resource for novice programmers. Companion files with code samples and figures are available for downloading from the publisher.

THE TARGET AUDIENCE

The book is intended to reach an international audience of readers with highly diverse backgrounds in various age groups. While many readers know how to read English, their native spoken language is not English (which could be their second, third, or even fourth language). Consequently, this book uses standard English rather than colloquial expressions that might be confusing to those readers. As you know, many people learn by different types of imitation, which includes reading, writing, or hearing new material. This book takes these points into consideration in order to provide a comfortable and meaningful learning experience for the intended readers.

GETTING THE MOST FROM THIS BOOK

Some programmers learn well from prose, others learn well from sample code (and lots of it), which means that there's no single style that can be used for everyone.

Moreover, some programmers want to run the code first, see what it does, and then return to the code to delve into the details (and others use the opposite approach).

Consequently, the code samples contain a mixture of short code samples and slightly longer code samples, whereas lengthy code samples are more suitable when you have acquired an understanding of the rudimentary features of Python 3.x.

WHY ARE SOFTWARE INSTALLATION INSTRUCTIONS NOT INCLUDED?

There are useful websites containing installation instructions for Python for various platforms. Instead of repeating those instructions in this book, that space is used for Python material. In general, this book attempts to avoid "filler" content as well as easily accessible set-up steps that are available online.

HOW WAS THE CODE FOR THIS BOOK TESTED?

The code samples in this book have been tested in Python version 3.9.1 on a MacBook Pro with OS X 10.8.5. Although you do not need the identical version of Python on your system, it's a good idea to have access to a version (e.g., Python 3.8) that is close to version 3.9.1.

WHAT DO I NEED TO KNOW FOR THIS BOOK?

The most useful prerequisite is some familiarity with another scripting language, which will familiarize you with basic programming concepts. Knowledge of a programming language such as Java can also be helpful for similar reasons (but it's not a requirement). However, keep in mind that the less technical knowledge that you have, the more diligence will be required in order to understand the various topics that are covered.

DOES THIS BOOK CONTAIN PRODUCTION-LEVEL CODE SAMPLES?

As mentioned earlier in the Preface, the primary purpose of the code samples in this book is to illustrate various features of Python 3.x. As such, code clarity has higher priority than writing more compact code that is more difficult to understand (and possibly more prone to bugs). If you decide to use any of the code in this book in a production environment, you ought to subject that code to the same rigorous analysis as the code in other parts of your application.

HOW DO I SET UP A COMMAND SHELL?

If you are a Mac user, there are three ways to do so. The first method is to use `Finder` to navigate to `Applications > Utilities` and then double click on the `Utilities` application. Next, if you already have a command shell available, you can launch a new command shell by typing the following command:

```
open /Applications/Utilities/Terminal.app
```

A second method for Mac users is to open a new command shell on a MacBook from a command shell that is already visible simply by clicking `command+n` in that command shell, and your Mac will launch another command shell.

If you are a PC user, you can install Cygwin (open source https://cygwin.com/) that simulates bash commands, or use another toolkit such as MKS (a commercial product). Please read the online documentation that describes the download and installation process. Note that custom aliases are not automatically set if they are defined in a file other than the main start-up file (such as .bash_login).

COMPANION FILES

Code samples and figures from the book are available by writing to the publisher at info@merclearning.com.

## CHAPTER 1

INTRODUCTION TO PYTHON

This chapter introduces Python, along with useful tools for installing its modules, working with its basic constructs, and handling some data types.

The first part of this chapter contains information about installing Python on your machine and how to launch the Python interpreter. This section includes code samples that you can save in text files to launch from the command line.

The second part of this chapter shows you how to work with simple data types, such as numbers and strings.

Before we start looking at code, keep in mind some of the chapters in this book contain "forward referencing" whereby a Python construct (such as a loop or a list) is used before it is discussed in detail in a subsequent chapter. For example, although conditional logic is discussed in Chapter 4, you will see a conditional code snippet in some examples. However, an if-else statement is easy to understand: when the "if" portion is true, execute some associated code; otherwise, execute the code in the "else" portion of the conditional logic. However, if the "forward referencing" code is too confusing, read the relevant material in a subsequent chapter and then return to the code sample in this chapter.

In addition, the latest production version of Python (as this book goes to print) is 3.11, which is significantly faster than 3.10 and 3.9, and Python 3.12 will be available soon. More information regarding Python 3.11 is accessible online:

https://www.i-programmer.info/news/216-python/15824-python-311-released.html

NOTE   *The Python scripts in this book are for Python 3.x.*

TOOLS FOR PYTHON

Although you only need Python installed on your machine for the code samples in this book, there are distributions available that include additional libraries. For example, the Anaconda Python distribution available for Windows, Linux, and Mac, and is downloadable: *http://continuum.io/downloads*.

Anaconda is well-suited for modules such as NumPy and SciPy, and if you are a Windows user, Anaconda appears to be a better alternative.

easy_install and pip

Both `easy_install` and `pip` are easy to use when you need to install Python modules. Whenever you need to install a module, use either `easy_install` or `pip` with the following syntax:

```
easy_install <module-name>
pip install <module-name>
```

NOTE *Python-based modules are easier to install, whereas modules with code written in C are usually faster, but more difficult to install.*

virtualenv

The `virtualenv` tool enables you to create isolated Python environments, and it is available online:

http://www.virtualenv.org/en/latest/virtualenv.html

`virtualenv` addresses the problem of preserving the correct dependencies and versions (and indirectly permissions) for different applications. (If you are a Python novice, you might not need `virtualenv` right now). The next section shows you how to check whether Python is installed on your machine, and where you can download Python.

PYTHON INSTALLATION

Before you download anything, check if you have Python already installed on your machine, which is likely if you have a MacBook or a Linux machine. Simply type the following command in a command shell:

```
python -V
```

The output for the MacBook used in this book is here:

```
python 3.9.1
```

NOTE *Install Python 3.9.1 (or as close as possible to this version) on your machine so that you will have the same version of Python that was used to test the code in this book.*

If you need to install Python on your machine, navigate to the Python home page and select the downloads link or navigate directly to this website:

http://www.python.org/download/

In addition, `PythonWin` is available for Windows, and its home page is online:

http://www.cgl.ucsf.edu/Outreach/pc204/pythonwin.html

Finally, use any text editor that can create, edit, and save Python scripts as plain text files (do not use Microsoft Word).

After you have Python installed and configured on your machine, you are ready to work with the files in this book.

SETTING THE PATH ENVIRONMENT VARIABLE (WINDOWS ONLY)

The PATH environment variable specifies a list of directories that are searched whenever you specify an executable program from the command line. A good guide to setting up your environment so that the executable is always available in every command shell is to follow the instructions found online:

http://www.blog.pythonlibrary.org/2011/11/24/python-101-setting-up-python-on-windows/

LAUNCHING PYTHON ON YOUR MACHINE

There are three different ways to launch Python:

• Use the Python Interactive Interpreter.
• Launch Python scripts from the command line.
• Use an IDE.

The next section shows you how to launch the interpreter from the command line. Later in this chapter, we show how to launch Python files from the command line.

NOTE *The emphasis in this book is to launch scripts from the command line, and in some cases, to enter code in the interpreter.*

The Python Interactive Interpreter

Launch the interactive interpreter from the command line by opening a command shell and typing the following command:

```
python
```

You will see the following prompt (or something similar):

```
Python 3.9.1 (v3.9.1:1e5d33e9b9, Dec  7 2020, 12:44:01)
[Clang 12.0.0 (clang-1200.0.32.27)] on darwin
Type "help", "copyright", "credits" or "license" for more information.
>>>
```

Type the expression 2 + 7 at the prompt:

```
>>> 2 + 7
```

Python displays the following result:

```
9
>>>
```

Press `ctrl-d` to exit the Python shell.

You can launch any Python script from the command line by preceding it with the word "`python`." For example, if you have the script `myscript.py` that contains Python statements, launch the script as follows:

```
python myscript.py
```

As a simple illustration, suppose that the Python file `myscript.py` contains the following code:

```
print('Hello World from Python')
print('2 + 7 = ', 2+7)
```

Launch the preceding code by typing `python myscript.py` from the command line, after which you will see the following output:

```
Hello World from Python
2 + 7 =  9
```

PYTHON IDENTIFIERS

A Python identifier is the name of a variable, function, class, module, or other object, and a valid identifier conforms to the following rules:

- starts with a letter A to Z, or a to z, or an underscore (_)
- zero or more letters, underscores, and digits (0 to 9)

NOTE *Python identifiers cannot contain characters such as @, $, and %.*

Python is a case-sensitive language, so "Abc" and "abc" are different identifiers.
In addition, Python has the following naming conventions:

- Class names start with an uppercase letter and all other identifiers with a lowercase letter.
- An initial underscore is used for private identifiers.
- Two initial underscores are used for strongly private identifiers.

An identifier with two initial underscores and two trailing underscores indicates a language-defined special name.

LINES, INDENTATIONS, AND MULTI-LINES

Unlike other programming languages (such as Java), Python uses indentation instead of curly braces for code blocks. Indentation must be consistent in a code block, as shown here:

```
if True:
    print("ABC")
    print("DEF")
```

```
else:
    print("ABC")
    print("DEF")
```

Multi-line statements can terminate with a new line or the backslash ("\") character, as shown here:

```
total = x1 + \
        x2 + \
        x3
```

You can place x1, x2, and x3 on the same line, so there is no reason to use three separate lines; however, this functionality is available in case you need to add a set of variables that do not fit on a single line.

You can specify multiple statements in one line by using a semicolon (";") to separate each statement, as shown here:

```
a=10; b=5; print(a); print(a+b)
```

The output of the preceding code snippet is as follows:

```
10
15
```

NOTE   *The use of semi-colons and the continuation character are discouraged in Python.*

QUOTATION MARKS AND COMMENTS

Python allows single ('), double ("), and triple (''' or """) quotation marks for string literals, provided that they match at the beginning and the end of the string. You can use triple quotation marks for strings that span multiple lines. The following examples are legal Python strings:

```
word = 'word'
line = "This is a sentence."
para = """This is a paragraph. This paragraph contains
more than one sentence."""
```

A string literal that begins with the letter "r" (for "raw") treats everything as a literal character and "escapes" the meaning of metacharacters:

```
a1 = r'\n'
a2 = r'\r'
a3 = r'\t'
print('a1:',a1,'a2:',a2,'a3:',a3)
```

The output of the preceding code block is as follows:

```
a1: \n a2: \r a3: \t
```

You can embed a single quotation mark in a pair of double quotation marks (and vice versa) to display a single quotation mark or double quotation marks. Another way to accomplish the same result is to precede a single or double quotation mark with a backslash ("\") character. The following code block illustrates these techniques:

```
b1 = "'"
b2 = '"'
b3 = '\''
b4 = "\""
print('b1:',b1,'b2:',b2)
print('b3:',b3,'b4:',b4)
```

The output of the preceding code block is as follows:

```
b1: ' b2: "
b3: ' b4: "
```

A hash sign (#) that is not inside a string literal is the character that indicates the beginning of a comment. Moreover, all characters after the # and up to the physical line end are part of the comment (and ignored by the interpreter). Consider the following code block:

```
# First comment
print("Hello, Python!")  # second comment
```

This code produces the following result:

```
Hello, Python!
```

A comment may be on the same line after a statement or expression:

```
name = "Tom Jones" # This is also a comment
```

You can comment multiple lines as follows:

```
# This is comment one
# This is comment two
# This is comment three
```

A blank line in Python is a line containing only whitespace, a comment, or both.

SAVING YOUR CODE IN A MODULE

Earlier you saw how to launch the interpreter from the command line and then enter Python statements. However, everything you type into the interpreter is only valid for the current session. If you exit the interpreter and then launch the interpreter again, your previous definitions are no longer valid. Fortunately, you can store Python code in a text file.

A *module* is a text file that contains Python statements. In the previous section, you saw how the interpreter enables you to test code snippets whose definitions are valid for the current session. If you want to retain the code snippets and other definitions, place them in a text file so that you can execute that code outside of the interpreter. One other detail to note is that modules are also called "scripts" in this book.

The outermost statements are executed from top to bottom when the module is imported for the first time, which will then set up its variables and functions. A module can be run directly from the command line, as shown here:

```
python first.py
```

As an illustration, place the following two statements in a text file called first.py:

```
x = 3
print(x)
```

Type the following command:

```
python first.py
```

The output from the preceding command is 3, which is the same as executing the preceding code from the interpreter.

SOME STANDARD MODULES

The Python Standard Library provides many modules that can simplify your own scripts. A list of the Standard Library modules is available online:

http://www.python.org/doc/

Some of the most important modules include cgi, math, os, pickle, random, re, socket, sys, time, and urllib.

The code samples in this book use the modules math, os, random, and re. You need to import these modules in order to use them in your code. For example, the following code block shows you how to import standard modules:

```
import re
import sys
import time
```

The code samples in this book import one or more of the preceding modules, as well as other Python modules.

THE help() AND dir() FUNCTIONS

An Internet search for Python-related topics usually returns a number of links with useful information. Alternatively, you can check the official documentation site: *docs.python.org*.

In addition, the help() and dir() functions are accessible from the interpreter. The help() function displays documentation strings, whereas the dir() function displays defined symbols. For example, if you type help(sys,) you see documentation for the sys module, whereas dir(sys) displays a list of the defined symbols.

Type the following command in the interpreter to display the string-related methods:

```
>>> dir(str)
```

The preceding command generates the following output:

```
['__add__', '__class__', '__contains__', '__delattr__', '__doc__',
'__eq__', '__format__', '__ge__', '__getattribute__', '__getitem__',
'__getnewargs__', '__getslice__', '__gt__', '__hash__', '__init__', '__
le__', '__len__', '__lt__', '__mod__', '__mul__', '__ne__', '__new__',
'__reduce__', '__reduce_ex__', '__repr__', '__rmod__', '__rmul__', '__
setattr__', '__sizeof__', '__str__', '__subclasshook__', '_formatter_
field_name_split', '_formatter_parser', 'capitalize', 'center', 'count',
'decode', 'encode', 'endswith', 'expandtabs', 'find', 'format', 'index',
'isalnum', 'isalpha', 'isdigit', 'islower', 'isspace', 'istitle',
'isupper', 'join', 'ljust', 'lower', 'lstrip', 'partition', 'replace',
'rfind', 'rindex', 'rjust', 'rpartition', 'rsplit', 'rstrip', 'split',
'splitlines', 'startswith', 'strip', 'swapcase', 'title', 'translate',
'upper', 'zfill']
```

The preceding list gives you a consolidated list of built-in functions. Although it is clear that the max() function returns the maximum value of its arguments, the purpose of other functions, such as filter() or map(), is not immediately apparent (unless you have used them in other programming languages). The preceding list provides a starting point for finding out more about various built-in functions that are not discussed in this chapter.

Note that while dir() does not list the names of built-in functions and variables, you can obtain this information from the standard module __builtin__ that is automatically imported under the name __builtins__:

```
>>> dir(__builtins__)
```

The following statement shows you how to get more information about a function:

```
help(str.lower)
```

The output from the preceding command is shown here:

```
Help on method_descriptor:

lower(...)
    S.lower() -> string

    Return a copy of the string S converted to lowercase.
(END)
```

Check the online documentation and also experiment with help() and dir() when you need additional information about a particular function or module.

COMPILE TIME AND RUNTIME CODE CHECKING

Python performs some compile-time checking for potential errors, but most checks (including type and name) are deferred until code execution. Consequently, if your code references a user-defined function that that does not exist, the code will compile successfully. In fact, the code will fail with an exception only when the code execution path references the non-existent function.

Although we discuss functions in a subsequent chapter, consider the following function myFunc that references the non-existent function called `DoesNotExist`:

```
def myFunc(x):
    if x == 3:
        print(DoesNotExist(x))
    else:
        print('x: ',x)
```

The preceding code only fails when the `myFunc` function is passed the value 3, after which Python raises an error. Later, we discuss how to define and invoke user-defined functions, along with an explanation of the difference between local versus global variables.

Now that you understand some basic concepts and how to launch your custom modules, the next section discusses ways to format data.

FORMATTING TECHNIQUES

Decimal numbers (such as 1.23 and 0.457) contain a decimal point that specify a combination of integer and decimal value. You can specify the number of decimal places of precision to use when printing decimal numbers:

```
>>> x = 1.23456
>>> format(x, '0.2f')
'1.23'
>>> format(x, '0.3f')
'1.235'
>>> 'value is {:0.3f}'.format(x) 'value is 1.235'
>>> from decimal import Decimal
>>> a = Decimal('4.2')
>>> b = Decimal('2.1')
>>> a + b
Decimal('6.3')
>>> print(a + b)
6.3
>>> (a + b) == Decimal('6.3')
True
>>> x = 1234.56789
>>> # Two decimal places of accuracy
>>> format(x, '0.2f')
'1234.57'
>>> # Right justified in 10 chars, one-digit accuracy
>>> format(x, '>10.1f')
' 1234.6'
>>> # Left justified
>>> format(x, '<10.1f') '1234.6'
>>> # Centered
>>> format(x, '^10.1f') ' 1234.6'
>>> # Inclusion of thousands separator
>>> format(x, ',')
'1,234.56789'
>>> format(x, '0,.1f')
'1,234.6'
```

Working with f-strings

Python supports several ways to print the value of a variable, and this section discusses f-strings, which is the most recent (and recommended) way to print the contents of a variable. Listing 1.1 displays the content of `fstrings1.py` that shows you how to display a numbers and strings using the "f" style in `print()` statements.

LISTING 1.1: fstrings1.py

```
import decimal

num1 = 12345
num2 = 12345.678
num3 = decimal.Decimal("1234.678")

print(f"num1: {num1}")
print(f"num1: {num1:3d}")
print(f"num1: {num1:5f}")
print(f"num1: {num1:.8f}")
print(f"num1: {num1:08}")
print(f"num1: {num1:,}")
print(f"num1: {f'${num1:.3f}':>10s}")
print(f'num1: {num3:{"4.3" if num3 < 100 else "8.3"}}')
print(f"square:{(lambda x: x**2)(15)}")
print(f"cube:  {(lambda x: x**3)(15)}")
print()


#error:
#print(f"num2: {num2:.3d}")
print(f"num2: {num2:.3f}")
print(f"num2: {num2:0.3f}")
print(f"num2: {num2:8.4f}")
print(f"num2: {num2:2.5f}")
```

Listing 1.1 contains an `import` statement, which you will often see in Python scripts because they provide additional functionality that is not part of the Python programming language. In this example, the `import` statement specifies `decimal`, which is used in one of the variables in this code sample.

The next portion of Listing 1.1 initializes the variables num1, num2, and num3 with decimal values, one of which involves the imported `decimal` library. Next, a block of `print()` statements displays the values of these three variables using different formats, followed by another block of `print()` statements that displays the contents of the variable num2 using different formats.

Listing 1.1 uses the "f-style" for printing variables, which you can understand by comparing the contents of each `print()` statement with its corresponding output. Launch the code in Listing 1.1, and you will see the following output:

```
num1: 12345
num1: 12345
num1: 12345.000000
num1: 12345.00000000
```

```
num1: 00012345
num1: 12,345
num1: $12345.000
num1:  1.23E+3
square:225
cube:  3375


num2: 12345.678
num2: 12345.678
num2: 12345.6780
num2: 12345.67800
```

Listing 1.2 displays the content of `fstrings2.py` that shows you how to display dates and text using the "f" style in `print()` statements.

LISTING 1.2: fstrings2.py

```python
import datetime

today = datetime.datetime.today()

print(f"today: {today}")
print(f"today: {today:%Y-%m-%d}")
print(f"today: {today:%Y}")
print(f"today: {today:%M}")
print(f"today: {today:%D}")
print()

text = "I love deep dish pizza"
print(f"text: {text}")
print(f"{text:^8}")

#error:
#print(f"text: {text:10f}")
#error:
#print(f"text: {text:10d}")
```

Listing 1.2 contains an `import` statement that specifies `datetime` instead of `decimal` because we need this library to initialize the variable `today` with today's date. The next portion of Listing 1.2 contains a block of `print()` statements that also use the "f-style" to print the contents of the variable `today` using different formats. As you can surmise, the letters Y, M, and D (and their lowercase counterparts) correspond to the year, month, and day, respectively, of a variable whose value is a legitimate date.

Another code snippet displays the contents of the variable `text` (which is a string) using two different formats. The final block is a "commented out" section of code that shows you invalid printing formats. Launch the code in Listing 1.2, and you will see the following output:

```
today: 2022-11-27 12:43:04.545559
today: 2022-11-27
today: 2022
```

```
today:  43
today:  11/27/22

text:  I love deep dish pizza
I love deep dish pizza
```

WORKING WITH STRINGS

Literal strings in Python 3 are based on Unicode by default, whereas earlier versions of Python used ASCII. Although Unicode and ASCII are not necessarily important for you to know right now, they are useful to learn because they occur in other programming languages. A simple Internet search will yield multiple free articles with detailed explanations.

You can concatenate two strings using the "+" operator. Launch Python from the command line by typing `python`, and then type the strings that are displayed inside a pair of quotation marks, starting with the following example that prints a string and then concatenates two single-letter strings:

```
>>> 'abc'
'abc'
>>> 'a' + 'b'
'ab'
```

You can use + or * to concatenate identical strings, as shown here:

```
>>> 'a' + 'a' + 'a'
'aaa'
>>> 'a' * 3
'aaa'
```

You can assign strings to variables and print them using the `print()` statement:

```
>>> print('abc')
abc
>>> x = 'abc'
>>> print(x)
abc
>>> y = 'def'
>>> print(x + y)
Abcdef
```

Comparing Strings

You can use the built-in methods `lower()` and `upper()` to convert a string to lowercase and uppercase, respectively:

```
>>> 'Python'.lower()
'python'
>>> 'Python'.upper()
'PYTHON'
>>>
```

The methods `lower()` and `upper()` are useful for performing a case insensitive comparison of two strings. Listing 1.3 shows the content of `compare1.py` that uses the `lower()` method to compare two strings.

LISTING 1.3: compare1.py

```
x = 'Abc'
y = 'abc'

if(x == y):
  print('x and y: identical')
elif (x.lower() == y.lower()):
  print('x and y: case insensitive match')
else:
  print('x and y: different')
```

Since x contains mixed case letters and y contains the same letters but in lowercase form, Listing 1.3 gives the following output:

```
x and y: case insensitive match
```

Two comments about Listing 1.3. First, Python (and many other languages) contain *methods*, which are similar to functions, and are discussed in more detail in Chapter 5. Second, the code contains a conditional block involving if/elif/else statements. Although conditional logic is discussed in more detail in Chapter 4, this code block is intuitive: "if […] is true, print something; otherwise, if […] is true, print something else; and if neither is true, then print another message."

FORMATTING STRINGS

This section contains a code block that has an import statement that imports the `string` library. We need this library so that we can invoke the methods `string.lstring()`, `string.rstring()`, and `string.center()` for positioning a text string so that it is left-justified, right-justified, and centered, respectively. As you saw in a previous section, the `format()` method exists for advanced interpolation features. Launch Python from the command line and then enter the following statements in the interpreter:

```
import string

str1 = 'this is a string'
print(string.ljust(str1, 10))
print(string.rjust(str1, 40))
print(string.center(str1,40))
```

The output is as follows:

```
this is a string
                        this is a string
            this is a string
```

SUMMARY

This chapter started with some Python tools, how to install Python, and how to launch Python on your machine. You also learned how to launch the Python interpreter and execute Python statements from inside the interpreter.

Next you learned about identifiers, indentation, and quotations and comments. In addition, you learned about standard modules, as well as `help()` and `dir()`. Then you learned about how to specify the number of decimal values to display in decimal numbers. You also saw how to work with strings, and also how to display strings as a left-justified or right-justified string.

## CHAPTER 2

STRING OPERATIONS

This chapter shows you how to work with strings in Python and perform various operations on strings, such as search and replace operations. This chapter will prepare you for the additional string-related tasks that are discussed in Chapter 6.

The first part of this chapter shows you how to "slice" and "splice" strings, as well as how to test for digits and alphabetic characters in a string.

The second part of this chapter shows you how to search and replace a string in other strings, and then how to remove leading and trailing characters. You will also see how to print text without the `newline` character and how to perform text alignment.

The third part of this chapter discusses dates and how to convert dates into strings. You will also learn how to handle user input and deal with exceptions.

Before you read this chapter, please keep in mind that you will see a mixture of code samples involving Python features that are discussed in more detail in subsequent chapters. In some cases, you will see functionality that is more advanced, such as that shown in the final section marked "optional." The intent is to make you aware of features in Python that you can follow up by reading online articles that describe their purpose.

WORKING WITH STRINGS

As you learned in Chapter 1, literal strings in Python 3 are Unicode by default. You can concatenate two strings using the "+" operator. The following example prints a string and then concatenates two single-letter strings:

```
>>> 'abc'
'abc'
>>> 'a' + 'b'
'ab'
```

You can use + or * to concatenate identical strings, as shown here:

```
>>> 'a' + 'a' + 'a'
'aaa'
>>> 'a' * 3
'aaa'
```

You can assign strings to variables and print them using the `print()` command:

```
>>> print('abc')
abc
>>> x = 'abc'
>>> print(x)
abc
>>> y = 'def'
>>> print(x + y)
Abcdef
```

You can "unpack" the letters of a string and assign them to variables, as shown here:

```
>>> str = "World"
>>> x1,x2,x3,x4,x5 = str
>>> x1
'W'
>>> x2
'o'
>>> x3
'r'
>>> x4
'l'
>>> x5
'd'
```

The preceding code snippets shows you how easy it is to extract the letters in a text string. You can also extract substrings of a string as shown in the following examples:

```
>>> x = "abcdef"
>>> x[0]
'a'
>>> x[-1]
'f'
>>> x[1:3]
'bc'
>>> x[0:2] + x[5:]
'abf'
```

However, your code will fail with an error if you attempt to subtract two strings:

```
>>> 'a' - 'b'
Traceback (most recent call last):
  File "<stdin>", line 1, in <module>
TypeError: unsupported operand type(s) for -: 'str' and 'str'
```

Fortunately, the `try/except` construct enables you to handle the preceding type of exception, as you will see in Chapter 3.

Formatting Strings

In Chapter 1, you saw examples of how to format strings. In addition, Python strings support the functions `ljust()`, `rjust()`, and `center()` for positioning a text string so that it is left-justified, right-justified, and centered, respectively. Enter the following statements in the interpreter:

```
import string

str1 = 'this is a string'
print(str1.ljust(10))
print(str1.rjust(40))
print(str1.center(40))
```

The output is as follows:

```
this is a string
                        this is a string
            this is a string
```

The next portion of this chapter shows you how to "slice" text strings by specifying ranges of characters in text strings.

SLICING AND SPLICING STRINGS

Python enables you to extract substrings of a string (called *slicing*) using array notation. Slice notation is `start:stop:step`, where the start, stop, and step values are integers that specify the start value, end value, and increment value, respectively. The default value for `step` is 1, and it is often omitted. The interesting part about slicing is that you can use the value –1, which operates from the right side instead of the left side of a string. Some examples of slicing a string are here:

```
text1 = "this is a string"
print('First 7 characters:',text1[0:7])
print('Characters 2-4:',text1[2:4])
print('Right-most character:',text1[-1])
print('Right-most 2 characters:',text1[-3:-1])
```

The output from the preceding code block is as follows:

```
First 7 characters: this is
Characters 2-4: is
Right-most character: g
Right-most 2 characters: in
```

As a teaser preview, here are some examples of how to specify subranges of Python lists (with more details in Chapter 5):

```
nums = [1,2,3,4,5,6,7]
v = nums[:3]
w = nums[3:]
x = nums[:-1]
y = nums[2:4]
z = nums[::-1]

str = "comprehension"
v = str[:3]
w = str[3:]
x = str[::3]
```

```
y = str[:-1]
z = str[::-1]

str = "RED"
y = 3*str
z = str*3
```

Testing for Digits and Alphabetic Characters

Python enables you to examine each character in a string and then test whether that character is a digit or an alphabetic character.

Listing 2.1 shows the content of char_types.py that illustrates how to determine whether a string contains digits or characters. (If you are unfamiliar with the conditional "if" statement in Listing 2.1, it is discussed in Chapter 4.)

LISTING 2.1: char_types.py

```
str1 = "4"
str2 = "4234"
str3 = "b"
str4 = "abc"
str5 = "a1b2c3"

if(str1.isdigit()):
  print("this is a digit:",str1)

if(str2.isdigit()):
  print("this is a digit:",str2)

if(str3.isalpha()):
  print("this is alphabetic:",str3)

if(str4.isalpha()):
  print("this is alphabetic:",str4)

if(not str5.isalpha()):
  print("this is not pure alphabetic:",str5)

print("capitalized first letter:",str5.title())
```

Listing 2.1 initializes some variables, followed by two conditional tests that check whether str1 and str2 are digits using the isdigit() function. The next portion of Listing 2.1 checks if str3, str4, and str5 are alphabetic strings using the isalpha() function. The output of Listing 2.1 is as follows:

```
this is a digit: 4
this is a digit: 4234
this is alphabetic: b
this is alphabetic: abc
this is not pure alphabetic: a1b2c3
capitalized first letter: A1B2C3
```

SEARCH FOR AND REPLACE A STRING IN OTHER STRINGS

Python provides methods for searching and replacing a string in a second text string. Listing 2.2 shows the content of find_pos1.py, which shows how to use the find() function to search for the occurrence of one string in another string.

LISTING 2.2: find_pos1.py

```
item1 = 'abc'
item2 = 'Abc'
text = 'This is a text string with abc'

pos1 = text.find(item1)
pos2 = text.find(item2)

print('pos1=',pos1)
print('pos2=',pos2)
```

Listing 2.2 initializes the variables item1, item2, and text, and then searches for the index of the contents of item1 and item2 in the string text. The find() function returns the column number where the first successful match occurs; otherwise, the find() function returns a -1 if a match is unsuccessful. The output from launching Listing 2.2 is here:

```
pos1= 27
pos2= -1
```

Listing 2.3 displays the content of replace1.py, which shows how to replace one string with another string.

LISTING 2.3: replace1.py

```
text = 'This is a text string with abc'
print('text:',text)
text = text.replace('is a', 'was a')
print('text:',text)
```

Listing 2.3 starts by initializing the variable text and then printing its contents. The next portion of Listing 2.3 replaces the occurrence of "is a" with "was a" in the string text, and then prints the modified string. The output from launching Listing 2.3 is as follows:

```
text: This is a text string with abc
text: This was a text string with abc
```

REMOVE LEADING AND TRAILING CHARACTERS

Python provides the functions strip(), lstrip(), and rstrip() to remove characters in a text string. Listing 2.4 shows the content of remove1.py, which gives the code for how to search for a string.

LISTING 2.4: remove1.py

```
text = '   leading and trailing white space   '
print('text1:','x',text,'y')

text = text.lstrip()
print('text2:','x',text,'y')

text = text.rstrip()
print('text3:','x',text,'y')
```

Listing 2.4 starts by concatenating the letter x and the contents of the variable `text`, and then printing the result. The second part of Listing 2.4 removes the leading white spaces in the string `text` and then appends the result to the letter x. The third part of Listing 2.4 removes the trailing white spaces in the string `text` (note that the leading white spaces have already been removed) and then appends the result to the letter x. The output from launching Listing 2.4 is here:

```
text1: x    leading and trailing white space    y
text2: x leading and trailing white space    y
text3: x leading and trailing white space y
```

If you want to remove extra white spaces inside a text string, use the `replace()` function as discussed in the previous section.

PRINTING TEXT WITHOUT NEWLINE CHARACTERS

If you need to suppress white space and a new line between objects output with multiple print statements, you can use concatenation or the `write()` function. The first technique is to concatenate the string representations of each object using the `str()` function prior to printing the result. For example, run the following statement:

```
x = str(9)+str(0xff)+str(-3.1)
print('x: ',x)
```

The output is shown here:

```
x:   9255-3.1
```

The preceding line contains the concatenation of the numbers 9 and 255 (which is the decimal value of the hexadecimal number 0xff) and -3.1.

Incidentally, you can use the `str()` function with modules and user-defined classes. An example involving the built-in module `sys` is as follows:

```
>>> import sys
>>> print(str(sys))
<module 'sys' (built-in)>
```

The following code snippet illustrates how to use the `write()` function to display a string:

```
import sys
write = sys.stdout.write
```

```
write('123')
write('123456789')
```

The output is here:

```
1233
1234567899
```

WORKING WITH DATES

Python provides a rich set of date-related functions, and this section provides one such example. Listing 2.5 shows the content of the script `datetime2.py`, which displays various date-related values, such as the current date and time; the day of the week, month, and year; and the time in seconds since the beginning of the epoch.

LISTING 2.5: datetime2.py

```
import time
import datetime

print("Time in seconds since the epoch: %s" %time.time())
print("Current date and time: " , datetime.datetime.now())
print("Or like this: " ,datetime.datetime.now().strftime("%y-%m-%d-%H-%M"))

print("Current year: ", datetime.date.today().strftime("%Y"))
print("Month of year: ", datetime.date.today().strftime("%B"))
print("Week number of the year: ", datetime.date.today().strftime("%W"))
print("Weekday of the week: ", datetime.date.today().strftime("%w"))
print("Day of year: ", datetime.date.today().strftime("%j"))
print("Day of the month : ", datetime.date.today().strftime("%d"))
print("Day of week: ", datetime.date.today().strftime("%A"))
```

Listing 2.6 displays the output generated by running the code in Listing 2.5.

LISTING 2.6: datetime2.out

```
Time in seconds since the epoch: 1375144195.66
Current date and time: 2023-07-29 17:29:55.664164
Or like this: 23-07-29-17-29
Current year: 2023
Month of year:  July
Week number of the year:  30
Weekday of the week:  1
Day of year:  210
Day of the month :  29
Day of week:  Monday
```

Python allows you to perform arithmetic calculations with date-related values, as shown in the following code block:

```
>>> from datetime import timedelta
>>> a = timedelta(days=2, hours=6)
>>> b = timedelta(hours=4.5)
>>> c = a + b
>>> c.days
2
>>> c.seconds
37800
>>> c.seconds / 3600
10.5
>>> c.total_seconds() / 3600
58.5
```

Converting Strings to Dates

Listing 2.7 shows the content of `string2date.py`, which illustrates how to convert a string to a date and how to calculate the difference between two dates.

LISTING 2.7: string2date.py

```
from datetime import datetime

text = '2024-08-13'
y = datetime.strptime(text, '%Y-%m-%d')
z = datetime.now()
diff = y - z
print('Date difference:',diff)
```

The output from Listing 2.7 is shown here:

```
Date difference: -210 days, 18:58:40.197130
```

EXCEPTION HANDLING

Chapter 1 mentioned that `try/except` blocks are useful for handling exceptions in Python, and this section contains more details regarding exceptions. As a side comment, JavaScript allows you to add numbers and strings, whereas you cannot add a number and a string in Python.

However, you can "catch" an attempt to add a number and a string via the `try/except` construct, which is similar to the `try/catch` construct in languages such as JavaScript and Java. An example of a `try/except` block for handling an error involving the addition of a number and a string is here:

```
try:
  x = 4
  y = 'abc'
  z = x + y
except:
  print 'cannot add incompatible types:', x, y
```

When you run the preceding code, the `print()` statement in the `except` code block is executed because the variables x and y have incompatible types.

As you saw earlier in the chapter, subtracting two strings is not supported in Python, and attempting to do so will result in an exception:

```
>>> 'a' - 'b'
Traceback (most recent call last):
  File "<stdin>", line 1, in <module>
TypeError: unsupported operand type(s) for -: 'str' and 'str'
```

A simple way to handle this situation is to use a `try/except` block:

```
>>> try:
...    print('a' - 'b')
... except TypeError:
...    print('TypeError exception while trying to subtract two strings')
... except:
...    print('Exception while trying to subtract two strings')
...
```

The output from the preceding code block is as follows:

```
TypeError exception while trying to subtract two strings
```

The preceding code block specifies the finer-grained exception called `TypeError`, followed by a "generic" `except` code block to handle all other exceptions that might occur during the execution of your code. (This style is similar to the exception handling in Java code.)

Listing 2.8 shows the content of `exception1.py`, which illustrates how to handle various types of exceptions.

LISTING 2.8: exception1.py

```
import sys

try:
    f = open('myfile.txt')
    s = f.readline()
    i = int(s.strip())
except IOError as err:
    print("I/O error: {0}".format(err))
except ValueError:
    print("Could not convert data to an integer.")
except:
    print("Unexpected error:", sys.exc_info()[0])
    raise
```

Listing 2.8 contains a `try` block followed by three `except` statements. If an error occurs in the `try` block, the first `except` statement is compared with the type of exception that occurred. If there is a match, then the subsequent `print` statement is executed, and the program terminates. If not, a similar test is performed with the second `except` statement. If neither `except` statement matches the exception, the third `except` statement handles the exception, which involves printing a message and then "raising" an exception.

Note that you can also specify multiple exception types in a single statement, as shown here:

```
except (NameError, RuntimeError, TypeError):
    print('One of three error types occurred')
```

The preceding code block is more compact, but you do not know which of the three error types occurred. Python allows you to define custom exceptions, but this topic is beyond the scope of this book.

HANDLING USER INPUT

Python enables you to read user input from the command line via the `input()` function or the `raw_input()` function. Typically, you assign user input to a variable that contains all the characters that users enter from the keyboard. User input terminates when users press the `<return>` key (which is included with the input characters). Listing 2.9 displays the content of `user_input1.py` that prompts users for their name and then uses interpolation to display a response.

LISTING 2.9: user_input1.py

```
userInput = input("Enter your name: ")
print ("Hello %s, my name is Python" % userInput)
```

The output of Listing 2.10 is as follows (assume that the user entered the word `Dave`):

```
Hello Dave, my name is Python
```

The `print()` statement in Listing 2.9 uses string interpolation via `%s`, which substitutes the value of the variable after the `%` symbol. This functionality is obviously useful when you want to specify something that is determined at run-time. User input can cause exceptions (depending on the operations that your code performs), so it is important to include exception-handling code.

Listing 2.10 shows the content of `user_input2.py`, which prompts users for a string and attempts to convert the string to a number in a `try/except` block.

LISTING 2.10: user_input2.py

```
userInput = input("Enter something: ")

try:
  x = 0 + eval(userInput)
  print('you entered the number:',userInput)
except:
  print(userInput,'is a string')
```

Listing 2.10 adds the number `0` to the result of converting a user's input to a number. If the conversion was successful, a message with the user's input is displayed. If the conversion failed, the `except` code block consists of a `print` statement that displays a message.

NOTE   *This code sample uses the `eval()` function, which should be avoided so that your code does not evaluate arbitrary (and possibly destructive) commands.*

Listing 2.11 shows the content of `user_input3.py`, which prompts users for two numbers and attempts to compute their sum in a pair of `try/except` blocks.

LISTING 2.11: user_input3.py

```
sum = 0

msg = 'Enter a number:'
val1 = input(msg)

try:
  sum = sum + eval(val1)
except:
  print(val1,'is a string')
  exit()

msg = 'Enter a number:'
val2 = input(msg)

try:
  sum = sum + eval(val2)
except:
  print(val2,'is a string')
  exit()

print('The sum of',val1,'and',val2,'is',sum)
```

Listing 2.11 contains two `try` blocks, each of which is followed by an `except` statement. The first `try` block attempts to add the first user-supplied number to the variable `sum`, and the second `try` block attempts to add the second user-supplied number to the previously entered number.

An error message occurs if either input string is not a valid number; if both are valid numbers, a message is displayed containing the input numbers and their sum.

COMMAND-LINE ARGUMENTS (OPTIONAL)

Python provides a `getopt` module to parse command-line options and arguments, and the `sys` module provides access to any command-line arguments via the `sys.argv`. This serves two purposes:

- `sys.argv` is the list of command-line arguments.
- `len(sys.argv)` is the number of command-line arguments.

Here, `sys.argv[0]` is the program name: if the program is called `test.py`, it matches the value of `sys.argv[0]`.

Now you can provide input values for a program on the command line instead of providing input values by prompting users for their input. As an example, consider the script `test.py` shown here:

```
#!/usr/bin/python
import sys
print('Number of arguments:',len(sys.argv),'arguments')
print('Argument List:', str(sys.argv))
```

Run above script as follows:

```
python test.py arg1 arg2 arg3
```

This will produce following result:

```
Number of arguments: 4 arguments.
Argument List: ['test.py', 'arg1', 'arg2', 'arg3']
```

Listing 2.12 shows the content of hello.py, which illustrates how to use sys.argv to check the number of command line parameters.

LISTING 2.12: hello.py

```
import sys

def main():
  if len(sys.argv) >= 2:
    name = sys.argv[1]
  else:
    name = 'World'
  print('Hello', name)

# Standard boilerplate to invoke the main() function
if __name__ == '__main__':
    main()
```

Listing 2.12 defines the main() function that checks the number of command-line parameters. If this value is at least 2, then the variable name is assigned the value of the second parameter (the first parameter is hello.py), otherwise name is assigned the value Hello. The print() statement then prints the value of the variable name.

In brief, when a module is run directly, the special variable __name__ is set to __main__. You will often see the following type of code in a module:

```
if __name__ == '__main__':
    # do something here
    print('Running directly')
```

The preceding code snippet allows Python to determine whether a module was launched from the command line or imported into another module. The preceding code snippet is used in the final portion of Listing 2.12 to determine whether to execute the main() function.

SUMMARY

This chapter started by showing you how to "slice" and "splice" strings, as well as how to test for digits and alphabetic characters in a string. Next, you learned how to search and replace a string in other strings, and then how to remove leading and trailing characters.

Then you learned how to print text without a new line character and how to perform text alignment. In addition, you saw how to work with dates and how to convert dates into strings. In addition, you learned how to handle user input and deal with exceptions using a `try/except` block. Finally, you learned how to work with command line arguments.

## CHAPTER 3

WORKING WITH LOOPS

This chapter shows you various types of loops in Python, such as `for` loops and `while` loops. You will also see examples of nested loops.

The first part of this chapter explains the precedence of operators, followed by a section that contains reserved words (i.e., words that you cannot use as variables in your Python code).

The second part of this chapter briefly discusses lists and various operations that you can perform on lists. This material is helpful for code samples involving lists that are discussed in subsequent chapters.

The third part of this chapter discusses `for` loops, along with code samples that show you how to use a `try/except` code block in a `for` loop. You will also see an example of a nested loop.

The fourth section contains examples of `while` loops, such as determining whether a positive integer is a prime number.

PRECEDENCE OF OPERATORS

When you have an expression involving numbers, you might remember that multiplication ("*") and division ("/") have higher precedence than addition ("+") or subtraction ("−"). Exponentiation has even higher precedence than these four arithmetic operators.

However, instead of relying on precedence rules, it is simpler (as well as safer) to use parentheses. For example, `(x/y)+10` is more explicit than `x/y+10`, even though they are equivalent expressions.

As another example, the following two arithmetic expressions are the equivalent, but the second is less error prone than the first because the latter contains parentheses:

```
x/y+3*z/8+x*y/z-3*x
(x/y)+(3*z)/8+(x*y)/z-(3*x)
```

The following website contains precedence rules for operators in Python:

http://www.mathcs.emory.edu/~valerie/courses/fall10/155/resources/op_precedence.html

RESERVED WORDS

Every programming language has a set of reserved words, which is a set of words that cannot be used as identifiers, and Python is no exception. The reserved words are and, exec, not, assert, finally, or, break, for, pass, class, from, print, continue, global, raise, def, if, return, del, import, try, elif, in, while, else, is, with, except, lambda, and yield.

If you inadvertently use a reserved word as a variable, you will see an "invalid syntax" error message instead of a "reserved word" error message. For example, suppose you create a script test1.py with the following code:

```
break = 2
print('break =', break)
```

If you run the preceding code, you will see the following output:

```
File "test1.py", line 2
  break = 2
        ^
SyntaxError: invalid syntax
```

However, a quick inspection of the code reveals the fact that you are attempting to use the reserved word break as a variable.

WORKING WITH LISTS

Python supports a list data type, along with a rich set of list-related functions. Since lists are not typed, you can create a list of different data types, as well as multidimensional lists. The next several sections show you how to manipulate list structures.

Lists and Basic Operations

A list consists of comma-separated values enclosed in a pair of square brackets. The following examples illustrate the syntax for defining a list, as well as how to perform various operations on a list:

```
>>> list = [1, 2, 3, 4, 5]
>>> list
[1, 2, 3, 4, 5]
>>> list[2]
3
>>> list2 = list + [1, 2, 3, 4, 5]
>>> list2
[1, 2, 3, 4, 5, 1, 2, 3, 4, 5]
>>> list2.append(6)
>>> list2
[1, 2, 3, 4, 5, 1, 2, 3, 4, 5, 6]
>>> len(list)
5
>>> x = ['a', 'b', 'c']
>>> y = [1, 2, 3]
```

```
>>> z = [x, y]
>>> z[0]
['a', 'b', 'c']
>>> len(x)
3
```

You can assign multiple variables to a list, provided that the number and type of the variables match the structure. Here is an example:

```
>>> point = [7,8]
>>> x,y = point
>>> x
7
>>> y
8
```

The following example shows you how to assign values to variables from a more complex data structure:

```
>>> line = ['a', 10, 20, (2024,01,31)]
>>> x1,x2,x3,date1 = line
>>> x1
'a'
>>> x2
10
>>> x3
20
>>> date1
(2024, 1, 31)
```

If you want to access the year/month/date components of the `date1` element in the preceding code block, you can do so with the following code block:

```
>>> line = ['a', 10, 20, (2024,01,31)]
>>> x1,x2,x3,(year,month,day) = line
>>> x1
'a'
>>> x2
10
>>> x3
20
>>> year
2024
>>> month
1
>>> day
31
```

If the number and/or structure of the variables do not match the data, an error message is displayed, as shown here:

```
>>> point = (1,2)
>>> x,y,z = point
```

```
Traceback (most recent call last):
  File "<stdin>", line 1, in <module>
ValueError: need more than 2 values to unpack
```

If the number of variables that you specify is less than the number of data items, you will see an error message, as shown here:

```
>>> line = ['a', 10, 20, (2024,01,31)]
>>> x1,x2 = line
Traceback (most recent call last):
  File "<stdin>", line 1, in <module>
ValueError: too many values to unpack
```

Reversing and Sorting a List

The `reverse()` method reverses the contents of a list, as shown here:

```
>>> a = [4, 1, 2, 3]
>>> a.reverse()
[3, 2, 1, 4]
```

The `sort()` method sorts a list:

```
>>> a = [4, 1, 2, 3]
>>> a.sort()
[1, 2, 3, 4]
```

You can sort a list and then reverse its contents, as shown here:

```
>>> a = [4, 1, 2, 3]
>>> a.reverse(a.sort())
[4, 3, 2, 1]
```

Another way to reverse a list is as follows:

```
>>> L = [0,10,20,40]
>>> L[::-1]
[40, 20, 10, 0]
```

Keep in mind is that `reversed(array)` is an *iterable* (discussed in Chapter 10) and not a list. However, you can convert the reversed array to a list with this code snippet:

```
list(reversed(array)) or L[::-1]
```

WORKING WITH LOOPS

Python supports `for` loops, `while` loops, and `range()` statements. The following subsections contain code samples that illustrate how you can use each of these constructs.

Python for Loops

Python supports the `for` loop that has a syntax that is slightly different from other languages (such as JavaScript and Java). The following code block shows you how to use a `for` loop in Python to iterate through the elements in a list:

```
>>> x = ['a', 'b', 'c']
>>> for w in x:
...     print(w)
...
a
b
c
```

The preceding code snippet prints three letters on three separate lines. You can force the output to be displayed on the same line (which will "wrap" if you specify a large enough number of characters) by appending a comma "," in the print() statement, as shown here:

```
>>> x = ['a', 'b', 'c']
>>> for w in x:
...     print(w,)
...
a b c
```

You can use this type of code when you want to display the contents of a text file in a single line instead of multiple lines.

Python also provides the built-in reversed() function that reverses the direction of the loop, as shown here:

```
>>> a = [1, 2, 3, 4, 5]
>>> for x in reversed(a):
... print(x)
5
4
3
2
1
```

Note that reversed iteration only works if the size of the current object can be determined or if the object implements a __reversed__() special method (also called a "magic method").

Listing 3.1 displays the content of for_loops1.py that illustrates various ways to use a for loop in Python.

LISTING 3.1: for_loops1.py

```
x = ['a', 'b', 'c']
for w in x:
  print(w,end=" 7 ")
print()

str = "Thick Pizza"
for c in str:
  print("char:",c)
print()

for c in str:
  print(c,end=" ")
print()
```

```
for c in str:
  print(w,end=" ")
print()

for i in range(len(str)):
  print(f"i:{i} char: {str[i]}")
print()
```

Listing 3.1 initializes the variable x as a list with three strings, followed by a loop that prints the elements in the variable x.

The next portion of Listing 3.1 contains another loop that iterates through the characters in the string str. The third and fourth for loops iterate through the characters in the string str and the variable w, respectively, and display their values.

The final portion of Listing 3.1 contains a for loop that iterates through the characters in the string str. Notice the use of the range() function for specifying a range of integers, as well as the len() function that returns the length of a string. In this code block, the range() function specifies the numbers in the range of 0 to len(str)-1, inclusive. Launch the code in Listing 3.1, and you will see the following output:

```
a 7 b 7 c 7
char: T
char: h
char: i
char: c
char: k
char:
char: P
char: i
char: z
char: z
char: a


T h i c k   P i z z a
c c c c c c c c c c c
i:0 char: T
i:1 char: h
i:2 char: i
i:3 char: c
i:4 char: k
i:5 char:
i:6 char: P
i:7 char: i
i:8 char: z
i:9 char: z
i:10 char: a
```

A for Loop with try/except

Listing 3.2 displays the content of string2nums.py that illustrates how to calculate the sum of a set of integers that have been converted from strings.

LISTING 3.2: string2nums.py

```
line = '1 2 3 4 10e abc'
sum  = 0
invalidStr = ""

print('String of numbers:',line)

for str in line.split(" "):
    try:
        sum = sum + eval(str)
    except:
        invalidStr = invalidStr + str + ' '

print('sum:', sum
if(invalidStr != ""):
  print('Invalid strings:',invalidStr)
else:
  print('All substrings are valid numbers')
```

Listing 3.2 initializes the variables `line`, `sum`, and `invalidStr`, and then displays the contents of line. The next portion of Listing 3.2 splits the contents of `line` into words, and then uses a `try` block to add the numeric value of each word to the variable sum. If an exception occurs, the content of the current `str` is appended to the variable `invalidStr`.

When the loop has finished execution, Listing 3.2 displays the sum of the numeric words, followed by the list of words that are not numbers. The output from Listing 3.2 is here:

```
String of numbers: 1 2 3 4 10e abc
sum: 10
Invalid strings: 10e abc
```

Flatten a List of Lists

Listing 3.3 displays the content of `flatten_list.py` that shows you how to flatten a list of lists.

LISTING 3.3: flatten_list.py

```
def flatten_extend(matrix):
    flat_list = []
    for row in matrix:
      flat_list.extend(row)
    return flat_list

matrix = [[1,2,3], [4,5,6],[7,8,9]]

result = flatten_extend(matrix)
print("original: ",matrix)
print("flattened:",result)
```

Listing 3.3 initializes the variable `flat_list` as an empty list, followed by the function `flatten_extend()` that contains a loop to process the contents of the argument matrix. During each iteration, the current item in `matrix` is appended to `flat_list` using the `extend()` method. After the loop has completed, the variable `flat_list` (which contains a flattened list) is returned. Keep in mind that the `append()` method appends a single item to a list, whereas the `extend()` method appends multiple items to a list.

The next portion of Listing 3.3 initializes the variable `matrix` and then invokes the function `flatten_extend()`, after which the original matrix and the flattened version are printed. Launch the code in Listing 3.3, and you will see the following output:

```
original:  [[1, 2, 3], [4, 5, 6], [7, 8, 9]]
flattened: [1, 2, 3, 4, 5, 6, 7, 8, 9]
```

Numeric Exponents in Python

Listing 3.4 displays the content of `nth_exponent.py` that illustrates how to calculate intermediate powers of a set of integers. Notice that the code contains a code snippet that starts with `def`, which is how to define custom functions in Python.

LISTING 3.4: nth_exponent.py

```
maxPower = 4
maxCount = 4

def pwr(num):
  prod = 1
  for n in range(1,maxPower+1):
    prod = prod*num
    print(num,'to the power',n, 'equals',prod)
  print('-----------')

for num in range(1,maxCount+1):
    pwr(num)
```

Listing 3.4 contains a function called `pwr()` that accepts a numeric value. This function contains a loop that prints the value of that number raised to the power n, where n ranges between 1 and `maxPower+1`.

The second part of Listing 3.4 contains a `for` loop that invokes the function `pwr()`, with the numbers between 1 and `maxPower+1`. The output from Listing 3.3 is here:

```
1 to the power 1 equals 1
1 to the power 2 equals 1
1 to the power 3 equals 1
1 to the power 4 equals 1
-----------
2 to the power 1 equals 2
2 to the power 2 equals 4
2 to the power 3 equals 8
2 to the power 4 equals 16
-----------
3 to the power 1 equals 3
3 to the power 2 equals 9
3 to the power 3 equals 27
3 to the power 4 equals 81
-----------
```

```
4 to the power 1 equals 4
4 to the power 2 equals 16
4 to the power 3 equals 64
4 to the power 4 equals 256
----------
```

NESTED LOOPS

Listing 3.5 displays the content of `triangular1.py` that illustrates how to print a row of consecutive integers (starting from 1), where the length of each row is one greater than the previous row.

LISTING 3.5: triangular1.py

```
max = 8
for x in range(1,max+1):
  for y in range(1,x+1):
    print(y,end="")
  print()
```

Listing 3.5 initializes the variable `max` with the value 8, followed by an outer `for` loop whose loop variable `x` ranges from 1 to `max+1`. The inner loop has a loop variable `y` that ranges from 1 to `x+1`. Moreover, the inner loop prints the value of `y` during each iteration. The output of Listing 3.5 is here:

```
1
1 2
1 2 3
1 2 3 4
1 2 3 4 5
1 2 3 4 5 6
1 2 3 4 5 6 7
1 2 3 4 5 6 7 8
```

WHILE LOOPS

You can define a `while` loop to iterate through a set of numbers, as shown in the following examples:

```
>>> x = 0
>>> while x < 5:
...     print(x
...     x = x + 1
...
0
1
2
3
4
5
```

Python uses indentation instead of curly braces, which are used in other languages, such as Java.

The following code block contains a variant of the preceding `while` loop that you can use when working with lists:

```
lst = [1,2,3,4]

while lst:
  print('list:',lst)
  print('item:',lst.pop())
```

The preceding `while` loop terminates when the `lst` variable is empty, and there is no need to explicitly test for an empty list. The output from the preceding code is here:

```
list: [1, 2, 3, 4]
item: 4
list: [1, 2, 3]
item: 3
list: [1, 2]
item: 2
list: [1]
item: 1
```

Count the Number of Digits in Numbers

Listing 3.6 displays the content of `n_exponent.py` that illustrates how to calculate intermediate powers of a set of integers. Notice that the code contains a code snippet that starts with `def`, which is how to define custom functions in Python.

LISTING 3.6: nth_exponent.py

```
maxPower = 4
maxCount = 4

def pwr(num):
  prod = 1
  for n in range(1,maxPower+1):
    prod = prod*num
    print(num,'to the power',n, 'equals',prod)
  print('-----------')

for num in range(1,maxCount+1):
    pwr(num)
```

Listing 3.6 starts by initializing two scalar variables and then defines the function `pwr()` containing a loop that ranges from 1 to `maxPower`, inclusive. During each iteration through the loop, the variable `prod` (which is initially 1) is multiplied by the value of the loop variable n. In addition, each intermediate calculation is printed.

The next portion of Listing 3.6 contains a loop that invokes the `pwr()` function with the values from 1 to `maxCount`, inclusive. Launch the code in Listing 3.6, and you will see the following output:

```
1 to the power 1 equals 1
1 to the power 2 equals 1
```

```
1 to the power 3 equals 1
1 to the power 4 equals 1
-----------
2 to the power 1 equals 2
2 to the power 2 equals 4
2 to the power 3 equals 8
2 to the power 4 equals 16
-----------
3 to the power 1 equals 3
3 to the power 2 equals 9
3 to the power 3 equals 27
3 to the power 4 equals 81
-----------
4 to the power 1 equals 4
4 to the power 2 equals 16
4 to the power 3 equals 64
4 to the power 4 equals 256
-----------
```

COUNT THE NUMBER OF DIGITS IN A POSITIVE INTEGER

Listing 3.7 shows you how to use a `while` loop to count the number of digits in a positive integer.

LISTING 3.7: count_digits_while.py

```python
def count_digits(num):
  count = 0
  while(num > 0):
    #print("new result:",result+1)
    #print("new number:",int(num/10))
    num = int(num/10)
    count += 1

  return count

numbers = [1234, 767, 1234321, 101]

for num in numbers:
  result = count_digits(num)
  print("Digits in ",num," = ",result)
```

Listing 3.7 starts with the function `count_digits()`, which contains a while loop that successively divides the argument `num` by 10 until the result is 0. Notice that the function `int()` is used to ensure that `num` is assigned an integer value. During each iteration, the scalar variable `count` (which is initially 0) is incremented, thereby counting the number of digits in `num`, after which the value of `count` is returned. Launch the code in Listing 3.7, and you will see the following output:

```
Digits in  1234  =  4
Digits in  767  =  3
Digits in  1234321  =  7
Digits in  101  =  3
```

USING A WHILE LOOP TO FIND THE DIVISORS OF A NUMBER

The code sample in this section contains a `while` loop, conditional logic, and the % (modulus) operator to find the factors of any integer greater than 1. Notice that this code sample contains a function called `divisors()`, even though functions are not discussed until Chapter 5. However, this user-defined function shows you the usefulness of defining functions that perform a set of calculations. In addition, if this example is not easy to understand, you can return to this code after you have read the material in Chapter 5.

LISTING 3.8: divisors.py

```
def divisors(num):
  div = 2

  while(num > 1):
    if(num % div == 0):
      print("divisor: ", div)
      num = num / div
    else:
      div = div + 1
  print("** finished **")

divisors(12)
```

Listing 3.8 defines a function `divisors()` that takes an integer value `num` and then initializes the variable `div` with the value 2. The `while` loop divides `num` by `div` and if the remainder is 0, it prints the value of `div` and then it divides `num` by `div`; if the value is not 0, then `div` is incremented by 1. This `while` loop continues as long as the value of `num` is greater than 1.

The output from Listing 3.7 passing in the value 12 to the function `divisors()` is here:

```
divisor:  2
divisor:  2
divisor:  3
** finished **
```

Listing 3.9 displays the content of `divisors2.py` that contains a `while` loop, conditional logic, and the % (modulus) operator to find the factors of any integer greater than 1.

LISTING 3.9: divisors2.py

```
def divisors(num):
  primes = ""
  div = 2
  divList = ""

  while(num > 1):
    if(num % div == 0):
      divList = divList + str(div) + ' '
      num = num / div
    else:
```

```
      div = div + 1
  return divList

result = divisors(12)
print('The divisors of',12,'are:',result)
```

Notice that Listing 3.9 is very similar to Listing 3.8: the main difference is that Listing 3.9 constructs the variable `divList` (which is a concatenated list of the divisors of a number) in the `while` loop, and then returns the value of `divList` when the `while` loop has completed. The output from Listing 3.9 is here:

```
The divisors of 12 are: 2 2 3
```

Using a while Loop to Find Prime Numbers

Listing 3.10 displays the content of `divisors3.py` that contains a `while` loop, conditional logic, and the % (modulus) operator to count the number of prime factors of any integer greater than 1. If there is only one divisor for a number, then that number is a prime number.

LISTING 3.10: divisors3.py

```
def divisors(num):
  count = 1
  div = 2

  while(div < num):
    if(num % div == 0):
      count = count + 1
    div = div + 1
  return count

result = divisors(12)

if(result == 1):
  print('12 is prime')
else:
  print('12 is not prime')
```

ASSIGNING VALUES TO MULTIPLE VARIABLES

Listing 3.11 displays the content of `multiple_vars.py` that illustrates how to assign values to multiple variables.

LISTING 3.11: multiple_vars.py

```
x,y,*z = range(7)
print("=> Group 1:")
print("x:",x)
print("y:",y)
print("z:",z)
print()
```

```
x,*y,z = range(7)
print("=> Group 2:")
print("x:",x)
print("y:",y)
print("z:",z)
print()

w = [*range(5)]
x = [*range(5),5]
y = [*range(5),5,6]
z = [*range(5),5,6,7]
print("=> Group 3:")
print("w:",w)
print("x:",x)
print("y:",y)
print("z:",z)
```

Listing 3.11 contains three "groups" of statements that initialize the variables x, y, and z in the first two groups and the variables w, x, y, and z in the third group.

The output of Listing 3.11 is here:

```
=> Group 1:
x: 0
y: 1
z: [2, 3, 4, 5, 6]

=> Group 2:
x: 0
y: [1, 2, 3, 4, 5]
z: 6

=> Group 3:
w: [0, 1, 2, 3, 4]
x: [0, 1, 2, 3, 4, 5]
y: [0, 1, 2, 3, 4, 5, 6]
z: [0, 1, 2, 3, 4, 5, 6, 7]
```

The main point to observe in Listing 3.11 is the "*" that appears in several variables, such as the variable z in the following snippet:

```
x,y,*z = range(7)
```

In simple terms, the variables x and y are assigned the first two values of range(7), which consists of the numbers 0 through 6 inclusive. The remaining values (i.e., 2 through 6, inclusive) are assigned to the variable z. However, the following code snippet generates an error:

```
x,y,z = range(7)
ValueError: too many values to unpack (expected 3)
```

THE break/continue/pass STATEMENTS

The break statement enables you to perform an "early exit" from a loop, whereas the continue statement essentially returns to the top of the loop and continues with the next value of the loop variable. The pass statement is essentially a "do nothing" statement.

Listing 3.12 displays the content of `break_continue_pass.py` that illustrates the use of these three statements.

LISTING 3.12: break_continue_pass.py

```
print('first loop')
for x in range(1,4):
  if(x == 2):
    break
  print(x)

print('second loop')
for x in range(1,4):
  if(x == 2):
    continue
  print(x)

print('third loop')
for x in range(1,4):
  if(x == 2):
    pass
  print(x)
```

The output of Listing 3.12 is here:

```
first loop
1
second loop
1
3
third loop
1
2
3
```

BASIC LIST COMPREHENSIONS

List comprehensions can perform any functionality that is possible with the `map()` and `filter()` functions, both of which are discussed in Chapter 11. Listing 3.13 displays the content of `comprehension1.py` that illustrates how to define comprehensions in Python.

LISTING 3.13: comprehension1.py

```
z = "AbCdEf!?@"
print("=> 1st z:",z)
nums = [ord(z) for z in z]
print("=> nums: ",nums)
print()
print("z is still AbCdEf:")
print("=> 2nd z:",z)
print()
```

```
nums = [ord(a) for a in z]
print("With a for loop:")
print("=> nums: ",nums)
print()
# a is *not* available

# with a "for" loop:
print("A for loop and conditional logic:")
nums = [ord(a) for a in z if ord(a) < 100]
print("=> nums: ",nums)
print()
```

WORKING WITH LIST COMPREHENSIONS

A list comprehension is a powerful construct that allows you to create a list of values in one line of code. Here is a simple example:

```
letters = [w for w in "Chicago Pizza"]
print(letters)
```

If you launch the preceding code snippet, you will see the following output:

```
['C', 'h', 'i', 'c', 'a', 'g', 'o', ' ', 'P', 'i', 'z', 'z', 'a']
```

As another example, consider the following two lines of code:

```
names1 = ["Sara","Dave","Jane","Bill","Elly","Dawn"]
names2 = [name for name in names1 if name.startswith("D")]
print("names2:",names2)
```

If you launch the preceding code snippet, you will see the following output:

```
names2: ['Dave', 'Dawn']
```

Another example involves a "for … for …" construct, as shown here:

```
names3 = ["Sara","Dave"]
names4 = [char for name in names3 for char in name]
```

If you launch the preceding code snippet, you will see the following output:

```
names3: ['Sara', 'Dave']
names4: ['S', 'a', 'r', 'a', 'D', 'a', 'v', 'e']
```

The following example illustrates a list comprehension that is an alternative to the map() function:

```
squared = [a*a for a in range(1,10)]
print("squared:",squared)
```

If you launch the preceding code snippet, you will see the following output:

```
squared: [1, 4, 9, 16, 25, 36, 49, 64, 81]
```

The following example illustrates a list comprehension that is an alternative to the `filter()` function:

```
evens = [a for a in range(1,10) if a%2 == 0]
print("evens:",evens)
```

If you launch the preceding code snippet, you will see the following output:

```
evens: [2, 4, 6, 8]
```

LISTS AND FILTER-RELATED OPERATIONS

Python enables you to filter a list via a list comprehension, as shown here:

```
mylist = [1, -2, 3, -5, 6, -7, 8]
pos = [n for n in mylist if n > 0]
neg = [n for n in mylist if n < 0]

print(pos)
print(neg)
```

You can also specify `if/else` logic in a filter, as shown here:

```
mylist = [1, -2, 3, -5, 6, -7, 8]
negativeList = [n if n < 0 else 0 for n in mylist]
positiveList = [n if n > 0 else 0 for n in mylist]

print(positiveList)
print(negativeList)
```

The output of the preceding code block is here:

```
[1, 3, 6, 8]
[-2, -5, -7]
[1, 0, 3, 0, 6, 0, 8]
[0, -2, 0, -5, 0, -7, 0]
```

SUMMARY

This chapter started with an explanation of the precedence of operators in Python, followed by a section that contains reserved words.

Next you learned about `for` loops, along with code samples that show you how to use a `try/except` code block in a `for` loop. You also saw an example of a nested loop.

In addition, you saw how to work with `while` loops, along with an example of finding the divisors of a positive integer. You learned how to check whether a positive integer is a prime number. Finally, you learned how to assign multiple values to multiple variables, and how to work with the keywords `break`, `continue`, and `pass`.

## CHAPTER 4

CONDITIONAL LOGIC

This chapter discusses conditional logic in Python. Virtually every Python program that performs useful calculations requires some type of conditional logic or control structure (or both). Although the syntax for these features is slightly different from other languages, the functionality will probably be familiar if you have worked with other scripting languages.

The first part of this chapter contains code samples that illustrate how to handle if-else conditional logic in Python, as well as if-elsif-else statements. This section also shows you how to determine whether a positive integer is a leap year.

The second part of this chapter discusses Boolean operators, such as in/not/is comparison operators, as well as and, or, and not operators.

The third section discusses local and global variables, as well as the scope of variables. In addition, you will also learn about passing by reference versus passing by value.

CONDITIONAL LOGIC

If you have written code in other programming languages, you are probably familiar with if/then/else (or if-elseif-else) conditional statements. Although the syntax varies between languages, the logic is essentially the same. The following example shows you how to use if/elif statements in Python:

```
>>> x = 25
>>> if x < 0:
...    print('negative')
... elif x < 25:
...    print('under 25')
... elif x == 25:
...    print('exactly 25')
... else:
...   print('over 25')
...
exactly 25
```

The preceding code block illustrates how to use multiple conditional statements.

CHECKING FOR LEAP YEARS

Listing 4.1 displays the content of `leap_years2.py` that shows you how to determine whether a given year is a leap year.

LISTING 4.1: leap_years2.py

```
# leap years are multiples of 4 except for
# centuries that are not multiples of 400

def check_year(year):
  if( year % 4 == 0 ):
    if( year % 100 == 0 ):
      if(year % 400 == 0):
        print(year, "is a leap year")
      else:
        print(year, "is not a leap year")
    else:
      print(year, "is a leap year")
  else:
    print(year, "is not a leap year")

years = [1234, 1900, 2000, 2020, 3000, 5588]

for year in years:
  check_year(year)
```

Listing 4.1 starts with the function `check_year()`, which uses an integer as its input parameter. The multiple conditional statements determine whether a given year is a leap year by implementing the description of a leap year that is provided in the two initial comment statements in this function.

The next portion of Listing 4.1 initializes the variable `years` as a list of positive integers, followed by a loop that iterates through the values of the variable `years`. During each iteration, this loop invokes the function `check_year()` with the current element in the variable `year`. Launch the code in Listing 4.1, and you will see the following output:

```
1234 is not a leap year
1900 is not a leap year
2000 is a leap year
2020 is a leap year
3000 is not a leap year
5588 is a leap year
```

COMPARISON AND BOOLEAN OPERATORS

Python supports a variety of Boolean operators, such as `in`, `not in`, `is`, `is not`, `and`, `or`, and `not`. The next several sections discuss these operators and provide some examples of how to use them.

The in/not in/is/is not Comparison Operators

The `in` and `not` in operators are used with sequences to check whether a value occurs in a sequence.

The operators `is` and `is not` determine whether or not two objects are the same object, which is important only matters for mutable objects such as lists. All comparison operators have the same priority, which is lower than that of all numerical operators.

Comparisons can be chained. For example, `a < b == c` tests whether a is less than b and moreover b equals c.

The and, or, and not Boolean Operators

The Boolean operators `and`, `or`, and `not` have lower priority than comparison operators. The Boolean `and` and `or` are binary operators whereas the Boolean `or` operator is a unary operator. Examples are here:

- `A and B` can only be true if both A and B are true
- `A or B` is true if either A or B is true
- `not(A)` is true if and only if A is false

You can also assign the result of a comparison or other Boolean expression to a variable, as shown here:

```
>>> string1, string2, string3 = '', 'b', 'cd'
>>> str4 = string1 or string2 or string3
>>> str4
'b'
```

The preceding code block initializes the variables `string1`, `string2`, and `string3`, where `string1` is an empty string. Next, `str4` is initialized via the `or` operator, and since the first non-null value is `string2`, the value of `str4` is equal to `string2`.

LOCAL AND GLOBAL VARIABLES

A variable is *local* to a function if it is:

- a parameter of the function
- on the left side of a statement in the function
- bound to a control structure (such as for, with, and except)

A variable that is referenced in a function, but is not local (according to the previous list) is a *non-local* variable. You can specify a variable as non-local with this snippet:

```
nonlocal z
```

A variable can be explicitly declared as *global* with this statement:

```
global z
```

Listing 4.2 displays the content of `global_local.py` that illustrates the behavior of a global versus a local variable.

LISTING 4.2: global_local.py

```
global z
z = 3

def changeVar(z):
  z = 4
  print('z in function:',z)

print('first global z:',z)

if __name__ == '__main__':
  changeVar(z)
  print('second global z:',z)
```

The output from the Listing 4.12 is here:

```
z in function: 4
first global z: 4
second global z: 3
```

Uninitialized Variables and the Value None

Python distinguishes between an uninitialized variable and the value None. The former is a variable that has not been assigned a value, whereas the value None is a value that indicates "no value." Collections and methods often return the value None, and you can test for the value None in conditional logic.

SCOPE OF VARIABLES

The accessibility or scope of a variable depends on where that variable has been defined. Python provides two scopes: global and local, with the added "twist" that global is actually module-level scope (i.e., the current file), and therefore you can have a variable with the same name in different files and they will be treated differently.

Local variables are defined inside a function, and they can only be accessed inside the function where they are defined.

Any variables that are not local variables have global scope, which means that those variables are "global" *only* with respect to the file where it has been defined, and they can be accessed anywhere in a file.

There are two scenarios to consider regarding variables. First, suppose two files (a.k.a., modules) file1.py and file2.py have a variable called x, and file1.py also imports file2.py. We must disambiguate between the x in the two different modules.

As an example, suppose that file2.py contains the following two lines of code:

```
x = 3
print('unscoped x in file2:',x)
```

Listing 4.3 displays the content of file1.py that imports file2.py.

LISTING 4.3: file1.py

```
import file2 as file2

x = 5
print('unscoped x in file1:',x)
print('scoped x from file2:',file2.x)
```

Launch file1.y from the command line, and you will see the following output:

```
unscoped x in file2: 3
unscoped x in file1: 5
scoped x from file2: 3
```

The second scenario involves a program containing a local variable and a global variable with the same name. According to the earlier rule, the local variable is used in the function where it is defined, and the global variable is used outside of that function.

Listing 4.4 displays the content of global_local2.py that shows you how to refer to a global variable and a local variable with the same name.

LISTING 4.4: global_local2.py

```
#!/usr/bin/python
# a global variable:
total = 0;

def sum(x1, x2):
    # this total is local:
    total = x1+x2;

    print("Local total : ", total)
    return total

# invoke the sum function
sum(2,3);
print("Global total : ", total
```

When the above code is executed, it produces following result:

```
Local total :   5
Global total :  0
```

What about *unscoped* variables, such as specifying the variable x without a module prefix? The answer consists of the following sequence of steps that Python will perform:

1. Check the local scope for the name.
2. Ascend the enclosing scopes and check for the name.
3. Perform Step #2 until the global scope is achieved (i.e., module level).
4. If x still has not been found, Python checks __builtins__.

Here is what this process looks like:

```
Python 3.9.1 (v3.9.1:1e5d33e9b9, Dec  7 2020, 12:44:01)
[Clang 12.0.0 (clang-1200.0.32.27)] on darwin
Type "help", "copyright", "credits" or "license" for more information.
>>> x = 1
>>> g = globals()
>>> g
{'g': {...}, '__builtins__': <module '__builtin__' (built-in)>, '__
package__': None, 'x': 1, '__name__': '__main__', '__doc__': None}
>>> g.pop('x')
1
>>> x
Traceback (most recent call last):
  File "<stdin>", line 1, in <module>
NameError: name 'x' is not defined
```

NOTE   *You can access the* `dicts` *that Python uses to track the local and global scope by invoking* `locals()` *and* `globals()`, *respectively.*

PASSING BY REFERENCE VERSUS BY VALUE

All arguments in the Python language are passed by reference to Python functions. Thus, if you change what a parameter refers to within a function, the change is reflected in the calling function. For example:

```
def changeme(mylist):
   "This changes a passed list into this function"
   mylist.append([1,2,3,4])
   print("Values inside the function: ", mylist)
   return


# Now you can call changeme function
mylist = [10,20,30]
changeme(mylist)
print("Values outside the function: ", mylist)
```

Here, we maintain the reference of the passed object and append the values in the same object; the result is shown here:

```
Values inside the function:  [10, 20, 30, [1, 2, 3, 4]]
Values outside the function:  [10, 20, 30, [1, 2, 3, 4]]
```

The fact that values are passed by reference gives rise to the notion of mutability versus immutability, which is discussed in Chapter 3.

ARGUMENTS AND PARAMETERS

Python differentiates between arguments to functions and parameter declarations in functions using a positional (mandatory) argument and keyword (the optional/default value). This concept is important because Python has operators for packing and unpacking these kinds of arguments. Python unpacks positional arguments from an iterable, as shown here:

```
>>> def foo(x, y):
...    return x - y
...
>>> data = 4,5
>>> foo(data) # only passed one arg
Traceback (most recent call last):
  File "<stdin>", line 1, in <module>
TypeError: foo() takes exactly 2 arguments (1 given)
>>> foo(*data) # passed however many args are in tuple
-1
```

SUMMARY

This chapter started with examples of if-else conditional logic, as well as if-elsif-else statements. You also learned how to use nested if statements to determine whether a positive integer is a leap year.

Next, you learned how to work with Boolean operators, such as in/not/is comparison operators, as well as and, or, and not operators.

Furthermore, you saw the difference between local and global variables, as well as the scope of variables. Finally, you learned about passing by reference versus passing by value.

## CHAPTER 5

BUILT-IN FUNCTIONS

T his chapter introduces you to Python built-in functions and how to define custom functions. If you have read the preceding chapters, you have already seen examples of defining custom functions. However, this chapter contains more extensive examples of functions. The first part of this chapter discusses the differences among functions and methods and then introduces various built-in functions; it contains examples of the split(), join(), and range() functions. You will also learn about the built-in char class, and how to use this class to determine whether a character is a digit or an alphabetic character.

The second section shows you examples of user-defined functions, and the third section shows you how to handle functions that return multiple values, as well as functions that have a variable number of parameters.

FUNCTIONS AND METHODS

In high-level terms, a *function* is a block of code that

- is called by name
- can be passed data to operate on (i.e., the parameters)
- can optionally return data (the return value)

All data that is passed to a function is explicitly passed. By contrast, a *method* is a block of code that

- is called by name
- is associated with an object

Based on the preceding statements, a method differs from a function in two ways:

- A method is implicitly passed the object for which it was called.
- A method is able to operate on data that is contained within the class.

BUILT-IN FUNCTIONS

Python provides an extensive list of built-in functions. The following list contains a subset of functions that are available in Python 3.x:

- `abs()`
- `bin()`
- `bool()`
- `chr()`
- `dict()`
- `enumerate(()`
- `filter()`
- `hash()`
- `int()`
- `len()`
- `map()`
- `max()`
- `min()`
- `ord()`
- `pow()`
- `rang()`
- `reversed()`
- `round()`
- `set()`
- `slice()`
- `str()`
- `sum()`
- `tuple()`
- `zip()`

Details about the functions in the preceding list (as well as additional built-in functions) is available online:

https://docs.python.org/3/library/functions.html

The split(), join(), and range() Functions

Some useful string-related built-in functions are listed here:

- `split()`
- `join()`
- `range()`

The `split()` function is useful when you want to tokenize ("split") a line of text into words, after which you can use a `for` loop to iterate through those words and process them accordingly. You saw various code samples in Chapter 3 that involve the built-in `split()` function.

The `join()` function does the opposite of `split()`: it "joins" two or more words into a single line. You can easily remove extra spaces in a sentence by using the `split()` function and then invoking the `join()` function, thereby creating a line of text with one white space between any two words.

The `range()` function is actually an iterator (discussed in Chapter 11) that enables you to generate a list of numbers, similar to a `for` loop. The syntax of the `range()` function is `range(start, stop, step)`, where `start` is the initial value, `stop` is the terminal value, and `step` is the increment (whose default value is 1).

The next several sections provide more information and code samples for these three functions.

THE join() FUNCTION

Another way to remove extraneous spaces is to use the `join()` function, as shown here:

```
text1 = '    there are      extra    spaces    '
print('text1:',text1)

text2 = ' '.join(text1.split())
print('text2:',text2)

text2 = 'XYZ'.join(text1.split())
print('text2:',text2)
```

The preceding code block contains a combination of the `split()` function and the `join()` function. First, the `split()` function "splits" a text string into a set of words, and also removes the extraneous white spaces. Next, the `join()` function "joins" together the words in the string `text1`, using a single white space as the delimiter. The last code portion of the preceding code block uses the string `XYZ` as the delimiter instead of a single white space.

The output of the preceding code block is here:

```
text1:    there are     extra   spaces
text2: there are extra spaces
text2: thereXYZareXYZextraXYZspaces
```

THE range() FUNCTION

This section contains examples of the `range()` function that you can use to iterate through the contents of a list, as shown here:

```
>>> for i in range(0,5):
...    print(i)
...
0
1
2
3
4
```

Of course, you can also use a `for` loop to iterate through a list of strings, as shown here:
```
>>> x
['a', 'b', 'c']
>>> for w in x:
...     print(w)
...
a
b
c
```

You can use a `for` loop to iterate through a list of strings and provide additional details, as shown here:
```
>>> x
['a', 'b', 'c']
>>> for w in x:
...     print(len(w), w)
...
1 a
1 b
1 c
```

The preceding output displays the length of each word in the list x, followed by the word itself.

THE CHAR CLASS

Listing 5.1 displays the content of the file `count_char_types.py` that counts the occurrences of digits and letters in a string.

LISTING 5.1: count_char_types.py

```
str1 = "abc4234AFde"
digitCount = 0
alphaCount = 0
upperCount = 0
lowerCount = 0

for i in range(0,len(str1)):
  char = str1[i]
  if(char.isdigit()):
   #print("this is a digit:",char)
    digitCount += 1
  elif(char.isalpha()):
   #print("this is alphabetic:",char)
    alphaCount  += 1
    if(char.upper() == char):
      upperCount  += 1
    else:
      lowerCount  += 1

print('Original String:   ',str1)
print('Number of digits:  ',digitCount)
```

```
print('Total alphanumeric:',alphaCount)
print('Upper Case Count:   ',upperCount)
print('Lower Case Count:   ',lowerCount)
```

Listing 5.1 initializes counter-related variables, followed by a loop (with loop variable i) that iterates from 0 to the length of the string str1. The string variable char is initialized with the letter at index i of the string str1. The next portion of the loop uses conditional logic to determine whether char is a digit or an alphabetic character; in the latter case, the code checks whether the character is uppercase or lower case. In all cases, the values of the appropriate counter-related variables are incremented.

The output of Listing 5.1 is here:

```
Original String:      abc4234AFde
Number of digits:     4
Total alphanumeric:   7
Upper Case Count:     2
Lower Case Count:     5
```

USER-DEFINED FUNCTIONS

The previous portion of this chapter discussed some built-in functions, and this section discusses how to define your own functions. You can define functions to provide the required functionality. Here are simple rules to define a function in Python:

- Function blocks begin with the keyword def, followed by the function name and parentheses.
- Any input arguments should be placed within these parentheses.
- The first statement of a function can be an optional statement - the documentation string of the function or docstring.
- The code block within every function starts with a colon (:) and is indented.
- The statement return [expression] exits a function, optionally passing back an expression to the caller. A return statement with no arguments is the same as return None.
- If a function does not specify the return statement, the function automatically returns None, which is a special type of value in Python.

A very simple custom function is here:

```
>>> def func():
...     print(3)
...
>>> func()
3
```

The preceding function is trivial, but it does illustrate the syntax for defining custom functions. The following example is slightly more useful:

```
>>> def func(x):
...     for i in range(0,x):
...         print(i)
```

```
. . .
>>> func(5)
0
1
2
3
4
```

THE return STATEMENT IN PYTHON FUNCTIONS

The `return` statement is not required in Python functions. Listing 5.2 displays the content of the file `func_return.py` that contains five functions with a `print()` statement and several functions that contain a `return` statement.

LISTING 5.2: func_return.py

```
def func1(x):
  print("func1:",x)

def func2(x):
  print("func2:",x)
  return

def func3(x):
  print("func3:",x)
  return x

def func4(x):
  return print("func4:",x)

def func5(x):
  print("func5: goodbye")
  return x

result1 = func1(7)
result2 = func2(7)
result3 = func3(7)
result4 = func4(7)
result5 = func5("hello")

print("result1:",result1)
print("result2:",result2)
print("result3:",result3)
print("result4:",result4)
print("result5:",result5)
```

Listing 5.2 contains several functions whose return type is `None`, which occurs in the functions that

- do not contain a `return` statement
- contain a `return` statement without an actual value
- contain a `return` statement that specifies a function that does not return a value

The first two items in the preceding are straightforward, but the third item might require additional explanation. Specifically, func4() contains a return statement that specifies a print() statement. However, a print() statement does *not* return a value: it simply prints whatever is specified inside the parentheses. Hence, func4() has a return type of None. Launch the code in Listing 5.2, and you will see the following output:

```
func1: 7
func2: 7
func3: 7
func4: 7
func5: goodbye
result1: None
result2: None
result3: 7
result4: None
result5: hello
```

SPECIFYING DEFAULT VALUES IN A FUNCTION

Listing 5.3 displays the content of default_values.py that illustrates how to specify default values in a function.

LISTING 5.3: default_values.py

```
def numberFunc(a, b=10):
  print(a,b)

def stringFunc(a, b='xyz'):
  print(a,b)

def collectionFunc(a, b=None):
  if(b is None):
     print('No value assigned to b')

numberFunc(3)
stringFunc('one')
collectionFunc([1,2,3])
```

Listing 5.3 defines three functions, followed by an invocation of each of those functions. The functions numberFunc() and stringFunc() print a list containing the values of their two parameters, and collectionFunc() displays a message if the second parameter is None. The output from Listing 5.3 is here:

```
(3, 10)
('one', 'xyz')
No value assigned to b
```

Returning Multiple Values from a Function

This task is accomplished by the code in Listing 5.4, which displays the contents of multiple_values.py.

LISTING 5.4: multiple_values.py

```
def MultipleValues():
    return 'a', 'b', 'c'

x, y, z = MultipleValues()

print('x:',x)
print('y:',y)
print('z:',z)
```

The output from Listing 5.4 is here:

```
x: a
y: b
z: c
```

FUNCTIONS WITH A VARIABLE NUMBER OF ARGUMENTS

Python enables you to define functions with a variable number of arguments. This functionality is useful in many situations, such as computing the sum, average, or product of a set of numbers. For example, the following code block computes the sum of two numbers:

```
def sum(a, b):
    return a + b

values = (1, 2)
s1 = sum(*values)
print('s1 = ', s1)
```

The output of the preceding code block is here:

```
s1 =  3
```

However, the sum function in the preceding code block can only be used for two numeric values.

Listing 5.5 displays the content of variable_sum1.py that illustrates how to compute the sum of a variable number of numbers.

LISTING 5.5: variable_sum1.py

```
def sum(*values):
    sum = 0
    for x in values:
        sum = sum + x
    return sum

values1 = (1, 2)
s1 = sum(*values1)
print('s1 = ',s1)
```

```
values2 = (1, 2, 3, 4)
s2 = sum(*values2)
print('s2 = ',s2)
```

Listing 5.5 defines the custom function `sum()`, whose parameter values can be an arbitrary list of numbers. The next portion of this function initializes `sum` to `0`, and then a `for` loop iterates through values and adds each of its elements to the variable `sum`. The last line in the function `sum()` returns the value of the variable `sum`. The output from Listing 5.5 is here:

```
s1 =   3
s2 =   10
```

One more detail to keep in mind: unlike other programming languages, Python allows you to define a custom function and a variable with the same name, such as the custom function `sum()` and the scalar variable `sum` in Listing 5.5.

IMPORTING CUSTOM MODULES

In addition to importing Python Standard Library modules, you can import your custom modules into other custom modules.

Listing 5.6 and Listing 5.7 display the contents of `Double.py` and `CallDouble.py` illustrating this functionality.

LISTING 5.6: Double.py

```
def double(num):
    return 2*num

result = double(5)
print('double 5 =', result)
```

Listing 5.6 defines the function `double()` that returns 2 times its argument, followed by the variable `result` that is assigned the value of `double(5)`. If you invoke Listing 5.6 from the Python interpreter or launch the program from the command line, you will see the following output:

```
double 5 = 10
```

LISTING 5.7: CallDouble.py

```
import Double
```

Listing 5.7 contains one line of code: an `import` statement that imports the `Double` module that is displayed in Listing 5.6. Launch Listing 5.7 from the command line and the output is shown here:

```
double 5 = 10
```

The combination of Listing 5.6 and Listing 5.7 demonstrate how easy it is to import a custom Python module. However, you obviously need the flexibility of invoking imported functions with different values.

Listing 5.8 and Listing 5.9 display the contents of `Triple.py` and `CallTriple.py` illustrating how to achieve this flexibility.

LISTING 5.8: Triple.py

```
def triple(num):
    return 3*num
```

Listing 5.8 contains only the definition of the function `triple()` that returns 3 times its argument, and there are no invocations of that function or any print statements.

LISTING 5.9: CallTriple.py

```
from Triple import triple

print('3 times 4 is:', triple(4))
print('3 times 9 is:', triple(9))
```

Launch Listing 5.9 from the command line, and you will see the following output:

```
3 times 4 is: 12
3 times 9 is: 27
```

Suppose that `Triple.py` also contained a function called `quadruple()`, and you wanted to import that function. You can do so with the following variation of the `import` statement:

```
from Triple import double, quadruple
```

If you want to import *all* the functions that are defined in `Triple.py`, use this form of the `import` statement:

```
from Triple import *
```

SUMMARY

This chapter started with a discussion of the differences among functions, methods, and classes. Then you learned about built-in functions, such as the `split()`, `join()`, and `range()` functions.

You also learned about the built-in `char` class, and how to use this class to determine whether a character is a digit or an alphabetic character.

In addition, you learned how to define custom functions, which are useful for creating modularized code. Furthermore, you saw how to work with functions that return multiple values, as well as functions that have a variable number of parameters.

## CHAPTER 6

TASKS WITH STRINGS AND ARRAYS

This chapter shows you how to perform various tasks involving bit values and strings. As you will see, the Python code samples in this chapter are more complex than the code samples in earlier chapters. Moreover, code samples in this chapter contain NumPy code, which is discussed in an appendix.

The first portion of this chapter shows you how to count word frequencies in an array of sentences.

The second portion of this chapter shows you how to find a common substring of two binary numbers, along with an example of counting word frequencies.

The third portion of this chapter shows you how to insert characters in a string, and then how to perform string permutations. The final example shows you how to determine whether a string is a palindrome.

TASK: COUNT WORD FREQUENCIES

Listing 6.1 displays the content of `word_frequency.py` that illustrates how to determine the frequency of each word in an array of words.

LISTING 6.1: word_frequency.py

```
import numpy as np

def word_count(words, check_word):
  count = 0
  for word in words:
    if(word.lower() == check_word.lower()):
      count += 1
  return count

sents = np.array([["I", "love", "thick", "pizza"],
                  ["I", "love", "deep", "dish","pizza"],
                  ["Pepperoni","and","sausage","pizza"],
                  ["Pizza", "with", "mozzarrella"]],dtype=object)
```

```
words = np.array([])
for sent in sents:
  for word in sent:
    words = np.append(words,word)

word_counts = {}
for word in words:
  count = word_count(words,word)
  word_counts[word] = count

print("word_counts:")
print(word_counts)
```

Listing 6.1 starts with the function word_count() that counts the number of occurrences of a given word in a sentence. The next portion of Listing 6.1 contains a loop that iterates through each sentence of an array of sentences. For each sentence, the code invokes the function word_count() with each word in the current sentence. Launch the code in Listing 6.1, and you will see the following output:

```
word_counts:
{'I': 2, 'love': 2, 'thick': 1, 'pizza': 4, 'deep': 1, 'dish': 1,
'Pepperoni': 1, 'and': 1, 'sausage': 1, 'Pizza': 4, 'with': 1,
'mozzarrella': 1}
```

Listing 6.2 displays the content of word_frequency2.py that illustrates another way to determine the frequency of each word in an array of words. Listing 6.2 uses a Python dictionary, which consists of name/value pairs. Note that other programming languages (such as Java) use the term *hash table* instead of dictionary.

Chapter 9 contains more information about managing a dictionary (such as creating a dictionary, deleting elements, and updating elements), which might be helpful for understanding the code in Listing 6.2.

LISTING 6.2: word_frequency2.py

```
import numpy as np

sents = np.array([["I", "love", "thick", "pizza"],
                  ["I", "love", "deep", "dish","pizza"],
                  ["Pepperoni","and","sausage","pizza"],
                  ["Pizza", "with", "mozzarrella"]],dtype=object)

word_counts = dict()
for sent in sents:
  for word in sent:
    word = word.lower()
    #print("word:",word)

    if(word not in word_counts.keys()):
        word_counts[word] = 0
    word_counts[word] += 1
```

```
print("word_counts:")
print(word_counts)
```

Listing 6.2 concatenates all the sentences and then populates a dictionary with word frequencies, whereas Listing 6.1 directly populates a dictionary with word frequencies. Launch the code in Listing 6.8, and you will see the following output:

```
word_counts:
{'i': 2, 'love': 2, 'thick': 1, 'pizza': 4, 'deep': 1, 'dish': 1,
'pepperoni': 1, 'and': 1, 'sausage': 1, 'with': 1, 'mozzarrella': 1}
```

TASK: CHECK IF A STRING CONTAINS UNIQUE CHARACTERS

Listing 6.3 displays the content of `unique_chars.py` that illustrates how to determine whether a string contains unique letters: note that the solution is for ASCII-based characters.

LISTING 6.3: unique_chars.py

```python
import numpy as np

def unique_chars(str):
  if (len(str) > 128):
    return false

  str = str.lower()

  char_set = np.zeros([128])

  for i in range (0,len(str)):
    char = str[i]
    val = ord('z') - ord(char)
    #print("val:",val)

    if (char_set[val] == 1):
      # found duplicate character
      return False
    else:
      char_set[val] = 1

  return True

arr1 = np.array(["a string", "second string", "hello world"])

for str in arr1:
  print("string:",str)
  result = unique_chars(str)
  print("unique:",result)
  print()
```

Listing 6.3 starts with the function `unique_chars()` that converts its parameter `str` to lowercase letters and then initializes the 1x128 integer array `char_set`, whose values are all 0. The next portion of this function iterates through the characters of the string `str` and initializes the integer variable `val` with the offset position of each character from the character "z."

If this position in `char_set` equals 1, then a duplicate character has been found; otherwise, this position is initialized with the value 1. Note that the value `False` is returned if the string `str` contains duplicate letters, whereas the value `True` is returned if the string `str` contains unique characters. Launch the code in Listing 6.3, and you will see the following output:

```
string: a string
unique: True

string: second string
unique: False

string: hello world
unique: False
```

TASK: INSERT CHARACTERS IN A STRING

Listing 6.4 displays the content of `insert_chars.py` that illustrates how to insert each character of one string in every position of another string.

LISTING 6.4: insert_chars.py

```
def insert_char(str1, chr):
  result = chr + str1
  for i in range(0,len(str1)):
    left = str1[:i+1]
    right = str1[i+1:]
    #print("left:",left,"right:",right)
    inserted = left + chr + right

    result = result + " " + inserted
  return result

str1 = "abc"
str2 = "def"
print("str1:",str1)
print("str2:",str2)

insertions = ""
for i in range(0,len(str2)):
  new_str = insert_char(str1, str2[i])
  #print("new_str:",new_str)
  insertions = insertions+ " " + new_str

print("result:",insertions)
```

Listing 6.4 starts with the function `insert_char()` that has a string `str1` and a character `chr` as input parameters. The next portion of code is a loop whose loop variable is `i`, which is used to split the string `str1` into two strings: the left substring from positions 0 to `i`, and the right substring from position `i+1`. A new string with three components is constructed: the left string, the character `chr`, and the right string.

The next portion of Listing 6.4 contains a loop that iterates through each character of `str2`; during each iteration, the code invokes `insert_char()` with string `str1` and the current character. The number of new strings generated by this code equals the following product: `(len(str1)+1)*len(str2)`.

Launch the code in Listing 6.4, and you will see the following output:

```
str1: abc
str2: def
result:  dabc adbc abdc abcd eabc aebc abec abce fabc afbc abfc abcf
```

TASK: STRING PERMUTATIONS

There are several ways to determine whether two strings are permutations of each other. One way involves sorting the strings alphabetically: if the resulting strings are equal, then they are permutations of each other.

A second technique is to determine whether they have the same number of occurrences for each character. A third way is to add the numeric counterpart of each letter in the string: if the numbers are equal and the strings have the same length, then they are permutations of each other.

Listing 6.5 displays the content of `string_permute.py` that illustrates how to determine whether two strings are permutations of each other.

LISTING 6.5: string_permute.py

```python
import numpy as np

def permute(str1,str2):
  str1d = sorted(str1)
  str2d = sorted(str2)
  permute = (str1d == str2d)

  print("string1: ",str1)
  print("string2: ",str2)
  print("permuted:",permute)
  print()

strings1 = ["abcdef", "abcdef"]
strings2 = ["efabcf", "defabc"]

for idx in range(0,len(strings1)):
  str1 = strings1[idx]
  str2 = strings2[idx]
  permute(str1,str2)
```

Listing 6.5 starts with the function `permute()` that takes the two strings `str1` and `str2` as arguments. Next, the strings `str1d` and `str2d` are initialized with the result of sorting the characters in the strings `str1` and `str2`, respectively. At this point, we can determine whether `str1` and `str2` are permutations of each other by checking whether the two strings `str1d` and `str2d` are equal. Launch the code in Listing 6.5, and you will see the following output:

```
string1:  abcdef
string2:  efabcf
permuted: False

string1:  abcdef
string2:  defabc
permuted: True
```

TASK: CHECK FOR PALINDROMES

One way to determine whether a given string is a palindrome is to compare the string with the reverse of the string: if the two strings are equal, then the string is a palindrome. Moreover, there are two ways to reverse a string: one way involves the `reverse()` function, and another way is to process the characters in the given string in a right-to-left fashion, and to append each character to a new string.

Another technique involves iterating through the characters in a left-to-right fashion and comparing each character with its corresponding character that is based on iterating through the string in a right-to-left fashion.

Listing 6.6 displays the content of `palindrome1.py` that illustrates how to determine whether a string or a positive integer is a palindrome.

LISTING 6.6: palindrome1.py

```python
import numpy as np

def palindrome1(str):
  full_len = int(len(str))
  half_len = int(len(str)/2)

  for i in range (0,half_len):
    lchar = str[i]
    rchar = str[full_len-1-i]
    if(lchar != rchar):
      return False
  return True

arr1 = np.array(["rotor", "tomato", "radar","maam"])
arr2 = list([123, 12321, 555])

# CHECK FOR STRING PALINDROMES:
for str in arr1:
  print("check string:",str)
  result = palindrome1(str)
  print("palindrome:  ",result)
  print()
```

```
# CHECK FOR NUMERIC PALINDROMES:
for num in arr2:
  print("check number:",num)
  str1 = np.str(num)
  str2 = ""
  for digit in str1:
    str2 += digit

  result = palindrome1(str2)
  print("palindrome:   ",result)
  print()
```

Listing 6.6 defines the function `palindrome1()`, which contains a loop that compares the elements from opposite directions of the string `str`. Specifically, the character in position 0 is compared with the right-most character of `str`: if they are different, then `str` is not a palindrome, and the value `False` is returned.

However, if the two characters are the same, then the process is repeated, this time with the character in position 1 and the character that is to the left of the right-most character of `str`. Repeat this process using the same conditional logic: if we reach the end of this loop, then `str` is a palindrome and the value `True` is returned.

The next portion of Listing 6.6 initializes the variables `arr1` and `arr2` with strings and numbers, respectively, followed by two loops. The first loop invokes the function `palindrome1()` with each element in `arr1`. The second loop initializes the string-based counterpart to each number in `arr2`, and then invokes the function `palindrome1()` with that string. Launch the code in Listing 6.6, and you will see the following output:

```
check string: rotor
palindrome:    True

check string: tomato
palindrome:    False

check string: radar
palindrome:    True

check string: maam
palindrome:    True

check number: 123
palindrome:    False

check number: 12321
palindrome:    True

check number: 555
palindrome:    True
```

WORKING WITH 1D ARRAYS

A *one-dimensional array* is a one-dimensional construct whose elements are homogeneous (i.e., mixed data types are not permitted). Given two arrays A and B, you can add or subtract them, provided that they have the same number of elements. You can also compute the inner product of two vectors by calculating the sum of their component-wise products.

Now that we have discussed some of the rudimentary operations with one-dimensional matrices, the following subsections illustrate how to perform various tasks on matrices.

Rotate an Array

Listing 6.7 displays the content of `rotate_list.py` that illustrates how to rotate the elements in a list.

LISTING 6.7: rotate_list.py

```python
list = [5,10,17,23,30,47,50]
print("original:",list)

shift_count = 2
for ndx in range(0,shift_count):
  item = list.pop(0)
  arr1 = list.append(item)

print("rotated: ",list)
```

Listing 6.7 initializes the variable `list` with a list of integers and prints its contents. The next portion of Listing 6.7 contains a loop that iterates from 0 to `shift_count` (initialized with the value 2), which is the number of times to shift the contents of the variable `list`. The shift is performed by invoking the `pop()` method to remove the left-most element of `list` and then immediately appending the "popped" element to the variable `list`. Launch the code in Listing 6.7, and you will see the following output:

```
original: [5, 10, 17, 23, 30, 47, 50]
rotated:  [17, 23, 30, 47, 50, 5, 10]
```

TASK: SORT ARRAY IN-PLACE WITHOUT A SORT FUNCTION

Listing 6.8 displays the content of `simple_sort.py` that illustrates a simple way to sort an array containing an *equal* number of values 0, 1, and 2 without using another data structure. The logic is simple: set the values of the elements in the first third of the array with the value 0, followed by an equal number of elements with the value 1, followed by an equal number of elements with the value 2.

LISTING 6.8: simple_sort.py

```python
arr1 = [0,1,2,2,1,0,0,1,2]
zeroes = 0

print("Initial:")
for i in range(0,len(arr1)):
    print(arr1[i],end=" ")
print()

for i in range(0,len(arr1)):
    if(arr1[i] == 0):
      zeroes += 1
```

```
third = int(len(arr1)/3)
for i in range(0,third):
   arr1[i]         = 0
   arr1[third+i]   = 1
   arr1[2*third+i] = 2

print("Sorted:")
for i in range(0,len(arr1)):
   print(arr1[i],end=" ")
print()
```

Listing 6.8 initializes arr1 with a list of multiple occurrences the values 0, 1, and 2, and then displays the contents of arr1. The second loop counts the number of occurrences the value 0 in the variable arr1. The third loop uses a "thirds" technique to assign the values 0, 1, and 2 to contiguous locations: all the 0 values appear first, followed by all the 1 values, and then all the 2 values. The key word in this task is "equal," which is shown in bold at the top of this section. Launch the code in Listing 6.8, and you will see the following output:

```
Initial:
0 1 2 2 1 0 0 1 2
Sorted:
0 0 0 1 1 1 2 2 2
```

TASK: INVERT ADJACENT ARRAY ELEMENTS

Listing 6.9 displays the content of invert_items.py that illustrates how to invert ("swap") adjacent pairs of elements in an array.

LISTING 6.9: invert_items.py

```
arr1 = [5,10,17,23,30,47,50]
print("original:",arr1)

mid_point = int(len(arr1)/2)

for ndx in range(0,mid_point+2,2):
  temp = arr1[ndx]
  arr1[ndx] = arr1[ndx+1]
  arr1[ndx+1] = temp

print("inverted:",arr1)
```

Listing 6.9 initializes the list arr1 and displays its contents. The next portion of Listing 6.9 contains a loop that uses the variable ndx to iterate from 0 to the midpoint of the array arr1.

During each iteration, the variable temp is initialized as the contents of the current element of arr1 to switch the values of the elements in arr1 in index positions ndx and ndx+1. Notice that the loop variable ndx is incremented by *two* instead of *one* because we are processing pairs of adjacent elements in arr1. Launch the code in Listing 6.9, and you will see the following output:

```
original: [ 5 10 17 23 30 47 50]
inverted: [10  5 23 17 47 30 50]
```

Listing 6.10 displays the content of swap.py that illustrates how to invert adjacent values in an array *without* using an intermediate temporary variable.

LISTING 6.10: swap.py

```
def swap(num1,num2):
  delta = num2 - num1
  #print("num1:",num1,"num2:",num2)

  num2 = delta
  num1 = num1+delta
  num2 = num1-delta
  #print("num1:",num1,"num2:",num2)
  return num1,num2

arr1 = [15,4,23,35,80,50]
print("BEFORE arr1:",arr1)

for idx in range(0,len(arr1),2):
  num1, num2 = swap(arr1[idx],arr1[idx+1])
  arr1[idx]   = num1
  arr1[idx+1] = num2
  #print("arr1:",arr1)

print("AFTER  arr1:",arr1)
```

Listing 6.10 defines the function swap() that swaps the values of two integer variables *without* using a loop. Perform a manual check with a pair of integers to confirm that swap() does indeed swap the values of its two parameters.

The next portion of Listing 6.10 initializes the list arr1, followed by a loop that iterates through adjacent pairs of elements of arr1. During each iteration, the function swap() is invoked, and the returned values are used to swap adjacent values in the array arr1. Launch the code in Listing 6.10, and you will see the following output:

```
BEFORE arr1: [15  4 23 35 80 50]
AFTER  arr1: [ 4 15 35 23 50 80]
```

WORKING WITH 2D ARRAYS

A *two-dimensional array* is a two-dimensional construct whose elements are homogeneous (i.e., mixed data types are not permitted). Given two arrays A and B, you can add or subtract them, provided that they have the same number of rows and columns.

Multiplication of matrices works differently from addition or subtraction: if A is an mxn matrix that you want to multiply (on the right of A) by B, then B must be an nxp matrix. The rule for matrix multiplication is as follows: the number of columns of A must equal the number of rows of B.

In addition, the *transpose* of matrix A is another matrix At such that the rows and columns are interchanged. Thus, if A is an mxn matrix then At is an nxm matrix. The matrix A is *symmetric* if A = At. The matrix A is the *identity matrix* I if the values in the main diagonal (upper left to lower right) are 1 and the other values are 0.

The matrix A is *invertible* if there is a matrix B such that A*B = B*A = I. Based on the earlier discussion regarding the product of two matrices, both A and B must be square matrices with the same number of rows and columns.

Now that we discussed some of the rudimentary operations with matrices, the following subsections illustrate how to perform various tasks on matrices.

THE TRANSPOSE OF A MATRIX

As a reminder, the transpose of matrix A is matrix At, where the rows and columns of A are the columns and rows, respectively, of matrix At.

Listing 6.11 displays the content of mat_transpose.py that illustrates how to find the transpose of an mxn matrix.

LISTING 6.11: mat_transpose.py

```
import numpy as np

# the transpose of a matrix is a 90 degree rotation
def transpose(A,rows,cols):
    for i in range(0,rows):
      for j in range(i,cols):
          #print("switching",A[i,j],"and",A[j,i])
          temp = A[i,j]
          A[i,j] = A[j,i]
          A[j,i] = temp
    return A

A = np.array([[100,3],[500,7]])
print("=> original:")
print(A)
At = transpose(A, 2, 2)
print("=> transpose:")
print(At)
print()


# example 2:
A = np.array([[100,3,-1],[30,500,7],[123,456,789]])
print("=> original:")
print(A)
At = transpose(A, 3, 3)
print("=> transpose:")
print(At)
```

Listing 6.11 defines the function transpose() that takes three parameters: an array A, the number of rows of A, and the number of columns of A. This function contains a nested loop that swaps the rows and columns of A, using a temporary variable temp whenever a swap is performed, to find (and return) the transpose of A.

The next portion of Listing 6.11 contains two examples of an array whose transpose is calculated via the function transpose(). Launch the code in Listing 6.11, and you will see the following output:

```
=> original:
[[100    3]
 [500    7]]
=> transpose:
[[100 500]
 [  3    7]]

=> original:
[[100    3   -1]
 [ 30  500    7]
 [123  456  789]]
=> transpose:
[[100   30  123]
 [  3  500  456]
 [ -1    7  789]]
```

In case you did not notice, the transpose At of a matrix A is actually a 90 degree rotation of matrix A. Hence, if A is a square matrix of pixels values for a PNG, then At is a 90 degree rotation of the PNG. However, if you take the transpose of At, the result is the original matrix A.

SUMMARY

This chapter started with an example of a set of positive integers and their binary representation. Next, you saw how to display binary substrings of a given integer.

In addition, you saw how to find a common substring of two binary numbers, along with an example of counting word frequencies.

Then you learned how to insert characters in a string and also how to perform string permutations. Finally, you saw how to determine whether a string is a palindrome.

## CHAPTER 7

TASKS WITH NUMBERS

This chapter shows you how to perform various tasks involving numbers and lists of numbers in Python.

The first part of this chapter contains a short introduction to time and complexity of algorithms, which involves concepts such as "big O" and "small O."

The second part of this chapter shows you how to calculate the sum of the even numbers and the sum of odd numbers in a list. You will also see how to calculate the number of digits in a positive integer.

The third part of this chapter shows you how to find the prime factorization of a positive integer. You will also learn how to verify Goldbach's conjecture for some small integers, which states that every even number greater than 2 is the sum of two prime numbers.

TIME AND SPACE COMPLEXITY

Algorithms are assessed in terms of the amount of space (based on input size) and the amount of time required for the algorithms to complete their execution, which is represented by "big O" notation. There are three types of time complexity: best case, average case, and worst case. An algorithm with a very good best case performance can have a relatively poor worst case performance.

Recall that $O(n)$ means that an algorithm executes in linear time because its complexity is bounded above and below by a linear function. For example, if three algorithms require $2*n$, $5*n$, or $n/2$ operations, then all of them have $O(n)$ complexity.

Moreover, if the best, average, and worst time performance for a linear search is 1, $n/2$, and n operations, respectively, then their complexity is $O(1)$, $O(n)$, and $O(n)$, respectively.

The *time-space trade-off* refers to reducing either the amount of time or the amount of memory that is required for executing an algorithm, which involves choosing one of the following:

- execute in less time and more memory
- execute in more time and less memory

Although reducing both time and memory is desirable, it is also a more challenging task. For example, the calculation of Fibonacci numbers is much more efficient via an iterative algorithm than a recursive solution, the former also requires an array to store intermediate values. Hence, the iterative solution has a higher memory requirement than a recursive solution.

Keep in mind is the following inequalities, where the logarithms can be in any base that is greater than or equal to 2, which holds for any positive integer n > 1:

```
O(log n) < O(n) < O(n*log n)
```

In addition, the following inequalities with powers of n, powers of 2, and factorial values are also valid:

```
O(n**2) < O(n**3) < O(2**n) < O(n!)
```

If you are unsure about any of the preceding inequalities, perform an online search for tutorials that provide the necessary details.

TASK: FIZZBUZZ

Listing 7.1 displays the content of fizz_buzz.py that shows you how to determine whether a number is a multiple of 3 or 5 or 15.

LISTING 7.1: fizz_buzz.py

```
numbers = [15,25,33,9,2]

for num in numbers:
  if num % 15 == 0:
    print(num,"is a multiple of 15")
  elif (num % 5 == 0):
    print(num,"is a multiple of 5")
  elif (num % 3 == 0):
    print(num,"is a multiple of 3")
  else:
    print(num,"is not a multiple of 3, 5, or 15")
```

Listing 7.1 starts by initializing the variable numbers as a list of positive integers, followed by a loop that processed each number in the numbers list. During each iteration, a block of conditional logic checks whether the current number is divisible by 15, by 5, by 3, or none of these integers, and an appropriate message is displayed. Launch the code in Listing 7.1, and you will see the following result:

```
15 is a multiple of 15
25 is a multiple of 5
33 is a multiple of 3
9 is a multiple of 3
2 is not a multiple of 3, 5, or 15
```

TASK: SUM OF EVEN AND ODD NUMBERS IN A LIST

Listing 7.2 displays the content of sum_even_odd.py that shows you how to calculate the sum of the even numbers and the sum of the odd numbers in a list.

LISTING 7.2: sum_even_odd.py

```
numbers = [1,10,101,52,300,-4]

odd_sum = 0
odd_cnt = 0
even_sum = 0
even_cnt = 0

for num in numbers:
  if(num % 2 == 0):
    #print("even:",num)
    even_sum += num
    even_cnt += 1
  else:
    #print("odd:",num)
    odd_sum += num
    odd_cnt += 1

print("Initial array:   ",numbers)
print("Sum of even #s:  ",even_sum)
print("Count of even #s:",even_cnt)
print("Sum of odd  #s:  ",odd_sum)
print("Count of odd  #s:",odd_cnt)
```

Listing 7.2 starts by initializing the variable `numbers` as a list of positive integers and also initializes some scalar variables with numeric values. Next, a loop iterates through the values in the `numbers` list. During each iteration, conditional logic checks if the current number is even: if so, then two scalar variables are incremented. However, if the current number is odd, then another pair of scalar variables is incremented.

The final portion of Listing 7.2 consists of a block of `print()` statements that display the values in the `numbers` list as well as the scalar variables that are initialized at the beginning of this code sample. Launch the code in Listing 7.2, and you will see the following result:

```
Initial array:    [1, 10, 101, 52, 300, -4]
Sum of even #s:    358
Count of even #s: 4
Sum of odd  #s:    102
Count of odd  #s: 2
```

TASK: MAXIMUM AND MINIMUM POWERS OF AN INTEGER

Listing 7.3 displays the content of `max_min_power_k2.py` that illustrates how to calculate the largest (smallest) power of a number whose base is k that is less than (greater than) a given number. So, if `num` and k are positive integers, the task is two-fold:

- find the *largest* number such that `k**powk <= num`
- find the *smallest* number such that `k**powk >= num`

For example, 16 is the *largest* power of two that is less than 24 and 32 is the *smallest* power of two that is greater than 24.

As another example, 625 is the largest power of five that is less than 1000 and 3125 is the smallest power of five that is greater than 1000.

LISTING 7.3: max_min_power_k2.py

```
def max_min_powerk(num,k):
  powk = 1
  while(powk <= num):
    powk *= k
  if(powk > num):
    powk /= k
  return int(powk), int(powk*k)

nums = [24,17,1000]
powers = [2,3,4,5]

for num in nums:
  for k in powers:
    upperk,lowerk = max_min_powerk(num, k)
    print("num:",num,"lower",lowerk,"upper:",upperk)
  print()
```

Listing 7.3 starts with the function `max_min_powerk()`, which contains a loop that repeatedly multiplies the local variable `powk` (initialized with the value 1) by `k`. When the value of `powk` is greater than the current value of `num`, `powk` is divided by `k` so that we have the lower bound solution.

Note that this function returns `powk` and `powk*k`, which represent the lower bound and higher bound solutions for this task. Launch the code in Listing 7.3, and you will see the following output:

```
num: 24 upper 16 lower: 32
num: 24 upper 9 lower: 27
num: 24 upper 16 lower: 64
num: 24 upper 5 lower: 25

num: 17 upper 16 lower: 32
num: 17 upper 9 lower: 27
num: 17 upper 16 lower: 64
num: 17 upper 5 lower: 25

num: 1000 upper 512 lower: 1024
num: 1000 upper 729 lower: 2187
num: 1000 upper 256 lower: 1024
num: 1000 upper 625 lower: 3125
```

TASK: CALCULATE THE NUMBER OF DIGITS

Listing 7.4 displays the content of `count_digits.py` that illustrates how to calculate the number of digits in positive integers. Note that this task is also solved via a `while` loop, as shown in Chapter 3. The code sample in this section gives you a preview of recursion, which is discussed in Chapter 11. If you are unfamiliar with recursion, you can return to this code sample after you have finished reading Chapter 11.

LISTING 7.4: count_digits.py

```
def count_digits(num, result):
  if(num == 0):
    return result
  else:
    #print("new result:",result+1)
    #print("new number:",int(num/10))
    return count_digits(int(num/10), result+1)

numbers = [1234, 767, 1234321, 101]

for num in numbers:
  result = count_digits(num, 0)
  print("Digits in ",num," = ",result)
```

Listing 7.4 starts with the function count_digits(), which recursively invokes itself with the term int(num/10), where num is the input parameter. Moreover, each invocation of count_digits() increments the value of the parameter result. Eventually, num will be equal to 0 (the terminating condition), at which point the value of result is returned.

If the logic of this code is not clear to you, try tracing through the code with the numbers 5, 25, 150, and you will see that the function count_digits() returns the values 1, 2, and 3, respectively. Launch the code in Listing 7.4, and you will see the following output:

```
Digits in  1234   =  4
Digits in  767   =  3
Digits in  1234321   =  7
Digits in  101   =  3
```

TASK: DETERMINE IF A POSITIVE INTEGER IS PRIME

Listing 7.5 displays the content of check_prime.py that illustrates how to calculate the number of digits in positive integers.

LISTING 7.5: check_prime.py

```
PRIME = 1
COMPOSITE = 0

def is_prime(num):
  div = 2

  while(div*div < num):
   if(num % div != 0):
     div += 1
   else:
      return COMPOSITE
  return PRIME

upperBound = 20
```

```
for num in range(2, upperBound):
  result = is_prime(num)
  if(result == True):
    print(num,": is prime")
  else:
    print(num,": is not prime")
```

Listing 7.5 starts with the function is_prime() that contains a loop that checks whether any integer in the range of 2 to sqrt(num) divides the parameter num, and then returns the appropriate result.

The second portion of Listing 7.5 contains a loop that iterates through the numbers from 2 to upperBound (which has the value 20) to determine which numbers are prime. Launch the code in Listing 7.5, and you will see the following output:

```
2 : is prime
3 : is prime
4 : is not prime
5 : is prime
6 : is not prime
7 : is prime
8 : is not prime
9 : is not prime
10 : is not prime
11 : is prime
12 : is not prime
13 : is prime
14 : is not prime
15 : is not prime
16 : is not prime
17 : is prime
18 : is not prime
19 : is prime
```

TASK: FIND THE PRIME FACTORIZATION OF A POSITIVE INTEGER

Listing 7.6 displays the content of prime_divisors.py that illustrates how to find the prime divisors of a positive integer.

LISTING 7.6: prime_divisors.py

```
PRIME = 1
COMPOSITE = 0

def is_prime(num):
  div = 2

  while(div < num):
    if(num % div != 0):
      div += 1
    else:
      return COMPOSITE

  #print("found prime:",num)
  return PRIME
```

```
def find_prime_divisors(num):
  div = 2
  prime_divisors = ""

  while(div <= num):
    prime = is_prime(div)

    if(prime == True):
      #print("=> prime number:",div)
      if(num % div == 0):
        prime_divisors += " "+str(div)
        num = int(num/div)
     else:
        div += 1
    else:
      div += 1


  return prime_divisors

upperBound = 20

for num in range(4, upperBound):
  result = find_prime_divisors(num)
  print("Prime divisors of ",num,":",result)
```

Listing 7.6 starts with the function is_prime() from Listing 7.6 that determines whether a positive integer is a prime number. Next, the function find_prime_divisors() contains a loop that iterates through the integers from 2 to num that checks which of those numbers is a prime number.

When a prime number is found, the code checks if that prime number is also a divisor of num: if so, that prime divisor is appended to the string prime_divisors . The final portion of Listing 7.6 returns the string prime_divisors that contains the prime factorization of the parameter num. Launch the code in Listing 7.6, and you will see the following output:

```
Prime divisors of  2 :  2
Prime divisors of  4 :  2 2
Prime divisors of  5 :  5
Prime divisors of  6 :  2 3
Prime divisors of  7 :  7
Prime divisors of  8 :  2 2 2
Prime divisors of  9 :  3 3
Prime divisors of  10 :  2 5
Prime divisors of  11 :  11
Prime divisors of  12 :  2 2 3
Prime divisors of  13 :  13
Prime divisors of  14 :  2 7
Prime divisors of  15 :  3 5
Prime divisors of  16 :  2 2 2 2
Prime divisors of  17 :  17
Prime divisors of  18 :  2 3 3
Prime divisors of  19 :  19
```

TASK: GOLDBACH'S CONJECTURE

Goldbach's conjecture states that every even number greater than 3 can be expressed as the sum of two odd prime numbers.

Listing 7.7 displays the content of `goldbach_conjecture.py` that illustrates how to determine a pair of prime numbers whose sum equals a given even number.

LISTING 7.7: goldbach_conjecture.py

```
PRIME = 1
COMPOSITE = 0

def prime(num):
  div = 2

  while(div < num):
   if(num % div != 0):
      div += 1
   else:
      return COMPOSITE
  return PRIME

def find_prime_factors(even_num):
  for num in range(3, int(even_num/2)):
    if(prime(num) == 1):
      if(prime(even_num-num) == 1):
        print(even_num , " = " , num , "+" , (even_num-num))

upperBound = 30

for num in range(4, upperBound):
  find_prime_factors(num)
```

Listing 7.7 also starts with the function `prime()`, which determines whether the parameter num is a prime number. Next, the function `find_prime_factors()` contains a loop whose loop variable num iterates from 3 to half the value of the variable even_num. If num is a prime number, then the conditional logic in Listing 7.7 invokes `prime()` with the number even_num-num.

If both num and even_num are prime, then they are a solution to Goldbach's conjecture because the sum of these two numbers equals the parameter even_num. Launch the code in Listing 7.7, and you will see the following output:

```
8   =   3 + 5
10  =   3 + 7
12  =   5 + 7
14  =   3 + 11
16  =   3 + 13
16  =   5 + 11
18  =   5 + 13
18  =   7 + 11
20  =   3 + 17
20  =   7 + 13
```

```
22  =  3 + 19
22  =  5 + 17
24  =  5 + 19
24  =  7 + 17
24  =  11 + 13
26  =  3 + 23
26  =  7 + 19
28  =  5 + 23
28  =  11 + 17
```

As you can see from the preceding output, the numbers 16, 18, 20, 22, 26, and 28 have two solutions to Goldbach's conjecture, and the number 24 has three such solutions.

TASK: SUM OF PRIME AND COMPOSITE NUMBERS

Listing 7.8 displays the content of `pair_sum_sorted.py` that illustrates how to determine whether a sorted array contains the sum of two specified numbers.

LISTING 7.8: pair_sum_sorted.py

```python
PRIME_NUM = 1
COMPOSITE = 0
prime_sum = 0
comp_sum  = 0

prime_list = []
comp_list  = []
arr1 = [5,10,17,23,30,47,50]

def is_prime(num):
  div = 2

  while(div < num):
   if(num % div != 0):
      div += 1
   else:
      return COMPOSITE
  return PRIME_NUM

for ndx in range(0,len(arr1)):
  num = arr1[ndx]

  if(is_prime(num) == PRIME_NUM):
    prime_list.append(num)
    prime_sum += num
  else:
    comp_list.append(num)
    comp_sum += num

print("prime list:",prime_list)
print("comp  list:",comp_list)
print("prime sum: ",prime_sum)
print("comp sum:  ",comp_sum)
```

Listing 7.8 starts with the function `is_prime()` that determines whether its input parameter is a prime number. The next portion of Listing 7.8 is a loop that ranges from 0 to the number of elements. During each iteration, the current number is added to the variable `prime_sum` if that number is a prime; otherwise, it is added to the variable `comp_sum`.

The final portion of Listing 7.8 displays the sum of the even numbers and the sum of the odd numbers in the input array `arr1`. Launch the code in Listing 7.6, and you will see the following output:

```
prime list: [5, 17, 23, 47]
comp  list: [10, 30, 50]
prime sum:  92
comp sum:   90
```

SUMMARY

This chapter started with an introduction to time and complexity of algorithms, which involves concepts such as "big O" and "small O."

Next, you saw how to calculate the sum of the even numbers and the sum of odd numbers in a list. You also learned how to calculate the number of digits in a positive integer.

In addition, you learned how to find the prime factorization of a positive integers, along with Goldbach's conjecture: every even number greater than 2 is the sum of two prime numbers.

## CHAPTER 8

WORKING WITH BIT VALUES

This book contains bit-related code samples for two reasons. First, bit-related code samples have a reputation for being complex and difficult to comprehend: in actuality, they do not deserve such a reputation. Second, some job interviews contain bit-related code questions, so a familiarity with these code samples has a practical use. However, you can treat these code samples as optional, and return to this chapter when you need to learn how to perform bit-related operations.

The first part of this chapter shows you how to print the binary representation of a sequence of integers, followed by an example of finding binary substrings of numbers.

The second portion shows you how to find a common substring of two binary numbers, how to invert bits in even and odd positions, and how to invert pairs of adjacent bits.

The third section shows you how to check if adjacent bits are set in a binary number and how to count bits in a range of numbers. You will also see how to find the right-most set bit in a number.

The final section shows you how to calculate the number of operations to make all characters equal, along with an example of how to compute the XOR of two numbers without using the XOR operator.

WORKING WITH BIT VALUES

Listing 8.1 displays the content of `binary_numbers.py` that illustrates how to display all binary substrings whose length is less than or equal to a given number.

LISTING 8.1: bit_values.py

```
numbers = range(0,17)

for num in numbers:
  print(f"number: {num:3} binary value: {bin(num):6}")
```

Listing 8.1 initializes the variable numbers with integers from 0 to 16 inclusive, followed by a loop that iterates through the values in the variable numbers. During each iteration, the current integer is printed, along with its binary representation. Launch the code in Listing 8.1, and you will see the following output:

```
number:    0 binary value: 0b0
number:    1 binary value: 0b1
number:    2 binary value: 0b10
number:    3 binary value: 0b11
number:    4 binary value: 0b100
number:    5 binary value: 0b101
number:    6 binary value: 0b110
number:    7 binary value: 0b111
number:    8 binary value: 0b1000
number:    9 binary value: 0b1001
number:   10 binary value: 0b1010
number:   11 binary value: 0b1011
number:   12 binary value: 0b1100
number:   13 binary value: 0b1101
number:   14 binary value: 0b1110
number:   15 binary value: 0b1111
number:   16 binary value: 0b10000
```

Let us consider several observations about the preceding output. First, Python uses a 0b prefix to indicate a binary number. Next, a number that is a power of 2 contains a left-most 1 that is followed by a set of 0 values. You can verify this fact by looking at the binary values for 2, 4, 8, and 16.

Third, a number that is one less than a power of 2 (such as 3, 7, and 15) have binary values consisting of only 1 value. As a result, you can determine whether a positive integer num is a power of two by performing an and operation between num and (num-1): if there are no bits with the value 1, then num is a power of two.

TASK: BINARY SUBSTRINGS OF A NUMBER

Listing 8.2 displays the content of binary_numbers.py that illustrates how to display all binary substrings whose length is less than or equal to a given number.

LISTING 8.2: binary_numbers.py

```
import numpy as np

def binary_values(width):
  print("=> binary values for width=",width,":")
  for i in range(0,2**width):
    bin_value = bin(i)
    str_value = str(bin_value)
    print(str_value[2:])
  print()

max_width = 4
for ndx in range(1,max_width):
  binary_values(ndx)
```

Listing 8.2 starts with the function `binary_values()` whose loop iterates from 0 to `2**width`, where `width` is the argument for this function. The loop variable is `i` and during each iteration, `bin_value` is initialized with the binary value of `i`.

Next, the variable `str_value` is the string-based value of `bin_value`, which is stripped of the two leading characters `0b`. Launch the code in Listing 8.2, and you will see the following output:

```
=> binary values for width= 1 :
0
1

=> binary values for width= 2 :
0
1
10
11

=> binary values for width= 3 :
0
1
10
11
100
101
110
111
```

TASK: COMMON 1 VALUES OF TWO BINARY NUMBERS

Listing 8.3 displays the content of `common_bits.py` that illustrates how to find the number of common 1 values of two binary strings.

LISTING 8.3: common_bits.py

```python
def common_bits(num1, num2):
    bin_num1 = bin(num1)
    bin_num2 = bin(num2)
    bin_num1 = bin_num1[2:]
    bin_num2 = bin_num2[2:]

    if(len(bin_num2) < len(bin_num1)):
      while(len(bin_num2) < len(bin_num1)):
        bin_num2 = "0" + bin_num2

    print(num1,"=",bin_num1)
    print(num2,"=",bin_num2)

    common_bits2 = 0
    for i in range(0,len(bin_num1)):
      if((bin_num1[i] == bin_num2[i]) and (bin_num1[i] =='1')):
        common_bits2 += 1
    return common_bits2
```

```
nums1 = [61,28, 7,100,189]
nums2 = [51,14,28,110, 14]

for idx in range(0,len(nums1)):
  num1 = nums1[idx]
  num2 = nums2[idx]
  common = common_bits(num1, num2)

  print(num1,"and",num2,"have",common,"bits in common")
  print()
```

Listing 8.3 starts with the function `common_bits()`, which initializes the binary numbers `bin_num1` and `bin_num2` with the binary values of the two arguments, after which the initial string "0b" is removed from both numbers.

Next, a loop iterates from 0 to the length of the string `bin_num1` to check each digit to see whether it equals 1. Each time the digit 1 is found, the value of `common_bits2` (initialized with the value 0) is incremented. When the loop terminates, the variable `common_bits2` equals the number of times that `bin_num1` and `bin_num2` have a 1 in the same position.

The final portion of Listing 8.3 iterates through a pair of arrays with positive integers values and invokes `common_bits()` during each iteration of the loop. Launch the code in Listing 8.3, and you will see the following output:

```
61 = 111101
51 = 110011
61 and 51 have 3 bits in common

28 = 11100
14 = 01110
28 and 14 have 2 bits in common

7 = 111
28 = 11100
7 and 28 have 3 bits in common

100 = 1100100
110 = 1101110
100 and 110 have 3 bits in common

189 = 10111101
14 = 00001110
189 and 14 have 2 bits in common
```

The next portion of this chapter contains various examples of string-related tasks. If need be, you can review the relevant portion of Chapter 1 regarding some of the built-in string functions, such as `int()` and `len()`.

TASK: INVERT BITS IN EVEN AND ODD POSITIONS

This solution to this task involves two parts: the first part "extracts" the bits in the even positions and shifts the result one bit to the right, followed by the second part that extracts the bits in the odd positions and shifts the result one bit to the right. Listing 8.4 displays the content of `swap_adjacent_bits.py` that illustrates how to solve this task.

LISTING 8.4: swap_adjacent_bits.py

```
# swap adjacent bits of a decimal number:
def swap(n):
  return ((n & 0xAAAAAAAA) >> 1) | ((n & 0x55555555) << 1)

arr1 = [70, 1000, 12341234]
for num in arr1:
  print("Decimal: ",num)
  print("Binary:   ",bin(num))
  print("Swapped: ",swap(num))
  print("Swapped: ",bin(swap(num)))
  print("-----------------\n")
```

Listing 8.4 defines the function `swap()` that returns the logical "or" of two strings. The first string is the logical "and" of the parameter n and a four-byte string consisting of the hexadecimal value A, after which this result is right-shifted by one bit. The second string is the logical "and" of the parameter n and a four-byte string consisting of the hexadecimal value 5, after which this result is left-shifted by one bit.

The following simplified example shows why the strings in the `swap()` function are the required values. Consider the decimal value 102 for the parameter n, whose binary value is 1111. Let's perform the operations in the `swap()` function, using two-byte hard-coded strings instead of their four-byte counterparts. Since the binary value of 102 equals 01100110, we have the following calculations:

```
n & 0xAA = 0110 0110 & 1010 1010 = 0010 0010
(n & 0XAA) >> 1 = 0010 0010 >> 1 = 0001 0001

n & 0x55 = 0110 0110 & 0101 0101 = 0100 0100
(n & 0x55) << 1 = 0100 & 0100 << 1 = 1000 1000

0001 0001 | 1000 1000 = 1001 1001
```

Compare the preceding code snippet shown in bold with the binary value of 102 and observe that the adjacent bit positions have been switched.

The next portion of Listing 8.4 contains a loop that iterates through the numbers in the list `arr1` in order to display their decimal values, as well as their "swapped" values. Launch the code in Listing 8.4, and you will see the following output:

```
Decimal:  70
Binary:   0b1000110
Swapped:  137
Swapped:  0b10001001
-----------------

Decimal:  1000
Binary:   0b1111101000
```

```
Swapped:   980
Swapped:   0b1111010100
----------------

Decimal:   12341234
Binary:    0b101111000100111111110010
Swapped:   8163313
Swapped:   0b11111001000111111110001
----------------
```

TASK: INVERT PAIRS OF ADJACENT BITS

This solution is similar to the code in the previous section, which also involves two parts: the "even" part extracts the bits in pairs of adjacent positions, starting from bit positions 2 and 3, and shifts the result two bits to the right, followed by the second part that extracts pairs of bits in the "odd" positions, starting from 0 and 1, and shifts the result two bits to the left. Listing 8.5 displays the content of swap_adjacent_pairs.py that illustrates how to solve this task.

LISTING 8.5: swap_adjacent_pairs.py

```
def swapAdjacentPairBits(num):
  # even mask: 11001100 => CC
  # odd mask:  00110011 => 33
  return ((num & 0xCCCC) >> 2) | ((num & 0x3333) << 2)

max = 200000
arr1 = [i for i in range(0,max)]

for num in arr1:
  swapped = swapAdjacentPairBits(num)
  bin1 = bin(swapped)[2:]
  dec1 = int(bin1, 2)

  print(f'Binary:  {bin(num):20} decimal: {num:8}')
  print(f'Swapped: {bin(swapped):20} decimal: {dec1:8}')
  print("")
```

Listing 8.5 generalizes the code in Listing 8.4: instead of swapping adjacent bits, the code in this section swaps *adjacent pairs* of bits. Hence, the function swapAdjacentPairBits() specifies the hard-coded strings 0xCCCC and 0x3333 (shown in bold), instead of 0xAAAA and 0x5555 that are specified in Listing 8.4. Launch the code in Listing 8.5, and you will see the following output:

```
Decimal:   70
Binary:    0b0             decimal:      0
Swapped:   0b0             decimal:      0

Binary:    0b1             decimal:      1
Swapped:   0b100           decimal:      4

Binary:    0b10            decimal:      2
Swapped:   0b1000          decimal:      8
```

```
Binary:  0b11                    decimal:      3
Swapped: 0b1100                  decimal:     12

Binary:  0b100                   decimal:      4
Swapped: 0b1                     decimal:      1
// output omitted for brevity
Binary:  0b110000110100111011 decimal:  199995
Swapped: 0b11111001110           decimal:   1998

Binary:  0b110000110100111100 decimal:  199996
Swapped: 0b11111000011           decimal:   1987

Binary:  0b110000110100111101 decimal:  199997
Swapped: 0b11111000111           decimal:   1991

Binary:  0b110000110100111110 decimal:  199998
Swapped: 0b11111001011           decimal:   1995

Binary:  0b110000110100111111 decimal:  199999
Swapped: 0b11111001111           decimal:   1999
```

At this point, we can generalize this code sample even further to reverse groups of four bits, where the "odd group" is the right-most four bits (with a binary mask of 00001111) and the "even group" is the left-most four bits (with a binary mask of 11110000). We now modify the code to switch adjacent triples of bits, and convert the binary masks to their corresponding hexadecimal values, which are 0F and F0, respectively.

We replace the masks in the swapAdjacentPairsBits() function in Listing 8.5 with the new pair of masks, and perform left and right shifts of 4 bits instead of 2, as shown here:

```
def swapAdjacentPairBits(num):
  # odd mask:   00001111 => OF
  # even mask: 11110000 => FO
  return ((num & 0xF0F0) >> 4) | ((num & 0x0F0F) << 4)
```

TASK: FIND COMMON BITS IN TWO BINARY NUMBERS

Listing 8.6 displays the content of common_bits.py that illustrates how to solve this task.

LISTING 8.7: common_bits.py

```
def common_bits(num1, num2):
    bin_num1 = bin(num1)
    bin_num2 = bin(num2)
    bin_num1 = bin_num1[2:]
    bin_num2 = bin_num2[2:]

    if(len(bin_num2) < len(bin_num1)):
      while(len(bin_num2) < len(bin_num1)):
        bin_num2 = "0" + bin_num2

    print(num1,"=",bin_num1)
    print(num2,"=",bin_num2)
```

```
      common_bits2 = 0
      for i in range(0,len(bin_num1)):
        if((bin_num1[i] == bin_num2[i]) and (bin_num1[i] =='1')):
          common_bits2 += 1
      return common_bits2

nums1 = [61,28, 7,100,189]
nums2 = [51,14,28,110, 14]

for idx in range(0,len(nums1)):
  num1 = nums1[idx]
  num2 = nums2[idx]
  common = common_bits(num1, num2)

  print(num1,"and",num2,"have",common,"bits in common")
  print()
```

Listing 8.6 defines the function `common_bits()` that initializes the variables `bin_num1` and `bin_num2` as the binary values for the parameters `num1` and `num2`, respectively. Notice that the first two index positions are skipped: this is necessary to exclude the string "0b" that appears in the binary values `bin_num1` and `bin_num2`.

The next portion of Listing 8.6 initializes the lists `nums1` and `nums2` with lists of positive integers, followed by a loop that iterates through these lists to determine the number of bits that are in common to each pair of array values. Launch the code in Listing 8.6, and you will see the following output:

```
61 = 111101
51 = 110011
61 and 51 have 3 bits in common

28 = 11100
14 = 01110
28 and 14 have 2 bits in common

7 = 111
28 = 11100
7 and 28 have 3 bits in common

100 = 1100100
110 = 1101110
100 and 110 have 3 bits in common

189 = 10111101
14 = 00001110
189 and 14 have 2 bits in common
```

TASK: CHECK FOR ADJACENT SET BITS IN A BINARY NUMBER

Listing 8.7 displays the content of `check_adjacent_bits.py` that illustrates how to solve this task.

LISTING 8.7: check_adjacent_bits.py

```
# true if adjacent bits are set in num:
def check(num):
  return num & (num << 1)

arr1 = [15, 16, 17, 50, 67, 99]
for num in arr1:
  print("Decimal: ",num)
  print("Binary:  ",bin(num))

  if check(num):
    print("Adjacent pair of set bits found")
  else:
    print("No adjacent pair of set bits found")
  print("---------------\n")
```

Listing 8.7 defines the function `check()` that returns the result of the logical "and" of the parameter n with the value (n<<1), which does detect the presence of adjacent bits that are set equal to 1. Launch the code in Listing 8.7, and you will see the following output:

```
15 in binary =  0b1111
Adjacent pair of set bits found
-----------------


16 in binary =  0b10000
No adjacent pair of set bits found
-----------------


17 in binary =  0b10001
No adjacent pair of set bits found
-----------------


50 in binary =  0b110010
Adjacent pair of set bits found
-----------------


67 in binary =  0b1000011
Adjacent pair of set bits found
-----------------


99 in binary =  0b1100011
Adjacent pair of set bits found
-----------------
```

TASK: COUNT BITS IN A RANGE OF NUMBERS

Listing 8.8 displays the content of `count_bits.py` that illustrates how to solve this task.

LISTING 8.8: count_bits.py

```
# Given an integer num, return an array of the number of 1's in
# the binary representation of every number in the range [0, num]

def count_bits(num):
  num_bin = bin(num)
  count = 0
  for i in range(0,len(num_bin)):
    if num_bin[i] == '1':
      count += 1
  #print(num,"has",count,"bits")
  return count

number = 20
total_bits = 0
bit_list = list()
for i in range(0,number):
  total_bits += count_bits(i)
  bit_list.append(count_bits(i))

print("=> Array of bit counts for numbers between 0 and",number,":")
print(bit_list)
```

Listing 8.8 defines the function `count_bits()`, which initializes the variable `num_bin` as the binary counterpart to the parameter `num`, followed by a loop that counts the number of occurrences of the string "1" in `num_bin`, whose value is returned by this function.

The next portion of Listing 8.8 initializes several variables, including the list variable `bit_list`, followed by a loop that counts the number of bits that appear in the numbers 0 through `number` (which is initialized with the value 20). Launch the code in Listing 8.8, and you will see the following output:

```
=> Array of bit counts for numbers between 0 and 20 :
[0, 1, 1, 2, 1, 2, 2, 3, 1, 2, 2, 3, 2, 3, 3, 4, 1, 2, 2, 3]
```

TASK: FIND THE RIGHT-MOST SET BIT IN A NUMBER

Listing 8.9 displays the content of `right_most_set_bit.py` that illustrates how to solve this task.

LISTING 8.9: right_most_set_bit.py

```
import numpy as np
import math

def getFirstSetBitPos(num):
  return math.log2(num & -num)+1

arr1 = np.array([12,18,29,66])
for num in arr1:
  bnum  = bin(num)
```

```
bnum2 = bnum[2:]
rbit  = (int(getFirstSetBitPos(num)))
#print(f'num: ",num," bnum: ",bnum," bnum2: ",bnum2," rbit: ",rbit)
print(f'num: {num:6} bnum: {bnum:10} bnum2: {bnum2:8} rbit: {rbit:6}')
```

Listing 8.9 defines the function `getFirstSetBitPos()` that returns 1 plus the logarithm (base 2) of the parameter `num` and the "and" of (`-num`). The next portion of Listing 8.9 initializes the variable `arr1` as a NumPy array of positive integers, followed by a loop that iterates through each value in `arr1`. The variable `bnum2` is initialized with the binary representation of num (which is an element of `arr1`), starting from index 2 to skip the string "0b."

Next, the variable bit is assigned as the integer result of invoking the function `getFirst-SetBitPos()` with the variable `num`, and then displays the values of `bnum`, `bnum2`, and `rbit`. Launch the code in Listing 8.9, and you will see the following output:

```
num:    12 bnum: 0b1100    bnum2: 1100     rbit:    3
num:    18 bnum: 0b10010   bnum2: 10010    rbit:    2
num:    29 bnum: 0b11101   bnum2: 11101    rbit:    1
num:    66 bnum: 0b1000010 bnum2: 1000010  rbit:    2
```

TASK: THE NUMBER OF OPERATIONS TO MAKE ALL CHARACTERS EQUAL

Listing 8.10 displays the content of `flip_bit_count.py` that illustrates how to solve this task.

LISTING 8.10: flip_bit_count.py

```
# determine the minimum number of operations
# to make all characters of the string equal
def minOperations(the_string):
  count = 0; # track the # of changes

  for i in range(1, len(the_string)):
    # are adjacent characters equal?
    if (the_string[i] != the_string[i - 1]):
      count += 1;

  return(count);

arr1 = ["0101010101", "1111010101", "100001", "111111"]
for str1 in arr1:
  print("String: ",str1)
  print("Result: ", minOperations(str1));
  print("----------------\n")
```

Listing 8.10 defines the function `minOperations()`, which contains a loop to count the number of times that adjacent characters (of a string) are different. This number equals the number of positions that must be "flipped" to make all characters equal.

The next portion of Listing 8.10 initializes the variable `arr1` as a list of strings that consist of either 0 or 1, followed by a loop that iterates through the elements of `arr1` and then invokes the function `minOperations()` to calculate the number of flips that are required. Launch the code in Listing 8.10, and you will see the following output:

```
String:  0101010101
Result:  9
----------------


String:  1111010101
Result:  6
----------------


String:  100001
Result:  2
----------------


String:  111111
Result:  0
----------------
```

TASK: COMPUTE XOR WITHOUT XOR FOR TWO BINARY NUMBERS

Listing 8.11 displays the content of `xor_without_xor.py` that illustrates how to solve this task.

LISTING 8.11: xor_without_xor.py

```python
# perform the XOR of two numbers without XOR:
def findBits(x, y):
  return (x | y) - (x & y)


arrx = [65,15]
arry = [80,240]

for idx in range(0,len(arrx)):
  x = arrx[idx]
  y = arry[idx]
  xory  = bin(x|y)
  xandy = bin(x&y)

  print("Decimal x: ",x)
  print("Decimal y: ",y)

  print("Binary x:  ",bin(x))
  print("Binary y:  ",bin(y))

  print("x OR y:    ",xory)
  print("x AND y:   ",xandy)
  print("x XOR y:   ",bin(findBits(x,y)))
  print("------------------\n")
```

Listing 8.11 defines the function findBits() that calculates the XOR value of its parameters x and y by computing (and returning) the quantity (x | y) - (x & y), which is logically equivalent to computing the XOR value of x and y. Launch the code in Listing 8.11, and you will see the following output:

```
Decimal x:   65
Decimal y:   80
Binary x:    0b1000001
Binary y:    0b1010000
x OR y:      0b1010001
x AND y:     0b1000000
x XOR y:     0b10001
------------------

Decimal x:   15
Decimal y:   240
Binary x:    0b1111
Binary y:    0b11110000
x OR y:      0b11111111
x AND y:     0b0
x XOR y:     0b11111111
------------------
```

SUMMARY

This chapter started by showing you how to print the binary representation of a sequence of integers, and then an example of finding binary substrings of a numbers. Next, you learned how to find a common substring of two binary numbers, how to invert bits in even and odd positions, and how to invert pairs of adjacent bits.

In addition, you saw how to check if adjacent bits are set in a binary number and how to count bits in a range of numbers. Moreover, you learned how to find the right-most set bit in a number.

You learned how to calculate the number of operations in order to make all characters equal. Finally, you learned how to compute the XOR of two numbers without using the XOR operator.

## CHAPTER 9

PYTHON DATA STRUCTURES

This chapter discusses Python data structures, such as sets, tuples, and dictionaries. You will see many short code blocks that will help you rapidly learn how to work with these data structures. After you have finished reading this chapter, you will be in a better position to create more complex modules using one or more of these data structures.

The first part of this chapter contains code samples involving lists and list comprehensions. The second part of this chapter discusses sets and how they differ from lists.

The third part of this chapter discusses tuples, and the final part of this chapter discusses dictionaries.

QUEUES

A queue is a FIFO ("First In, First Out") data structure. Thus, the oldest item in a queue is removed when a new item is added to a queue that is already full. (Queues are discussed in more detail in Chapter 5.) Although you can use a list to emulate a queue, there is also a queue object in Python. The following code snippets illustrate how to use a queue.

```
>>> from collections import deque
>>> q = deque('',maxlen=10)
>>> for i in range(10,20):
...     q.append(i)
...
>>> print(q)
deque([10, 11, 12, 13, 14, 15, 16, 17, 18, 19], maxlen=10)
```

TUPLES (IMMUTABLE LISTS)

Python supports a data type called a *tuple* that consists of comma-separated values either with or without brackets (square brackets are for lists, round brackets are for tuples, and curly braces are for dictionaries). Various examples of tuples can be found online:

https://docs.python.org/3.6/tutorial/datastructures.html#tuples-and-sequences

The following code block illustrates how to create a tuple and create new tuples from an existing type.

Define a tuple t as follows:

```
>>> t = 1,'a', 2,'hello',3
>>> t
(1, 'a', 2, 'hello', 3)
```

Display the first element of t:

```
>>> t[0]
1
```

Create a tuple v containing 10, 11, and t:
```
>>> v = 10,11,t
>>> v
(10, 11, (1, 'a', 2, 'hello', 3))
```

Try modifying an element of t (which is immutable):

```
>>> t[0] = 1000
Traceback (most recent call last):
  File "<stdin>", line 1, in <module>
TypeError: 'tuple' object does not support item assignment
```

Python *deduplication* is useful because you can remove duplicates from a set and obtain a list:

```
>>> lst = list(set(lst))
```

NOTE *The* in *operator on a list to search is* O(n), *whereas the* in *operator on set is* O(1).

SETS

A *set* is an unordered collection that does not contain duplicate elements. Use curly braces or the set() function to create sets. Set objects support set-theoretic operations such as union, intersection, and difference.

NOTE set() *is required to create an empty set because* {} *creates an empty dictionary.*

The following code snippets illustrate how to work with a set.
Create a list of elements:

```
>>> l = ['a', 'b', 'a', 'c']
```

Create a set from the preceding list:

```
>>> s = set(l)
>>> s
set(['a', 'c', 'b'])
```

Test if an element is in the set:

```
>>> 'a' in s
True
>>> 'd' in s
False
>>>
```

Create a set from a string:

```
>>> n = set('abacad')
>>> n
set(['a', 'c', 'b', 'd'])
>>>
```

Subtract n from s:

```
>>> s - n
set([])
```

Subtract s from n:

```
>>> n - s
set(['d'])
>>>
```

Create the union of s and n:

```
>>> s | n
set(['a', 'c', 'b', 'd'])
```

Create the intersection of s and n:

```
>>> s & n
set(['a', 'c', 'b'])
```

Find the exclusive-or of s and n:

```
>>> s ^ n
set(['d'])
```

DICTIONARIES

Python has a key/value structure called a "dict" that is a hash table. A Python dictionary (and hash tables in general) can retrieve the value of a key in constant time, regardless of the number of entries in the dictionary (and the same is true for sets).

You can think of a set as essentially just the keys (not the values) of a dict implementation. The contents of a dict can be written as a series of "key:value" pairs, as shown here:

```
dict1 = {key1:value1, key2:value2, ...}
```

The "empty dict" is just an empty pair of curly braces {}.

Creating a Dictionary

A dictionary (or hash table) contains of colon-separated key/value bindings inside a pair of curly braces, as shown here:

```
dict1 = {}
dict1 = {'x' : 1, 'y' : 2}
```

The preceding code snippet defines `dict1` as an empty dictionary, and then adds two key/value bindings.

Displaying the Contents of a Dictionary

You can display the contents of `dict1` with the following code:

```
>>> dict1 = {'x':1,'y':2}
>>> dict1
{'y': 2, 'x': 1}
>>> dict1['x']
1
>>> dict1['y']
2
>>> dict1['z']
Traceback (most recent call last):
  File "<stdin>", line 1, in <module>
KeyError: 'z'
```

NOTE *Key/value bindings for a* `dict` *and a set are not necessarily stored in the same order that you defined them.*

Python dictionaries also provide the `get` method to retrieve key values:

```
>>> dict1.get('x')
1
>>> dict1.get('y')
2
>>> dict1.get('z')
```

As you can see, the `get()` method returns `None` (which is displayed as an empty string) instead of an error when referencing a key that is not defined in a dictionary. You can also use `dict` comprehensions to create dictionaries from expressions, as shown here:

```
>>> {x: x**3 for x in (1, 2, 3)}
{1: 1, 2: 8, 3: 37}
```

Checking for Keys in a Dictionary

You can check for the presence of a key in a dictionary as follows:

```
>>> 'x' in dict1
True
>>> 'z' in dict1
False
```

Use square brackets for finding or setting a value in a dictionary. For example, `dict['abc']` finds the value associated with the key `'abc'`. You can use strings, numbers, and tuples work as key values, and you can use any type as the value.

If you access a value that is not in the `dict`, Python throws a `KeyError`. Consequently, use the "in" operator to check if the key is in the `dict`. Alternatively, use `dict.get(key)`, which returns the value or `None` if the key is not present. You can even use the expression `get(key, not-found-string)` to specify the value to return if a key is not found.

Deleting Keys from a Dictionary

Launch the interpreter, and enter the following commands:

```
>>> MyDict = {'x' : 5,   'y' : 7}
>>> MyDict['z'] = 13
>>> MyDict
{'y': 7, 'x': 5, 'z': 13}
>>> del MyDict['x']
>>> MyDict
{'y': 7, 'z': 13}
>>> MyDict.keys()
['y', 'z']
>>> MyDict.values()
[13, 7]
>>> 'z' in MyDict
True
```

Iterating Through a Dictionary

The following code snippet shows you how to iterate through a dictionary:

```
MyDict = {'x' : 5,   'y' : 7, 'z' : 13}

for key, value in MyDict.iteritems():
    print(key, value)
```

The output from the preceding code block is here:

```
y 7
x 5
z 13
```

Interpolating Data from a Dictionary

The `%` operator substitutes values from a dictionary into a string by name. Listing 9.3 displays the content of `interpolate_dict1.py` that shows you how to do so.

LISTING 9.3: interpolate_dict1.py

```
hash = {}
hash['beverage'] = 'coffee'
hash['count'] = 3
# %d for int, %s for string
s = 'Today I drank %(count)d cups of %(beverage)s' % hash
```

The output from the preceding code block is here:

```
Today I drank 3 cups of coffee
```

Dictionary Functions and Methods

Python provides various functions and methods for a dictionary, such as cmp(), len(), and str(), which compare two dictionaries, return the length of a dictionary, and display a string representation of a dictionary, respectively.

You can also manipulate the contents of a dictionary using the functions clear() to remove all elements, copy() to return a shall copy, get() to retrieve the value of a key, items() to display the (key, value) pairs of a dictionary, keys() to display the keys of a dictionary, and values() to return the list of values of a dictionary.

Dictionary Formatting

The % operator works to substitute values from dict into a string by name:

```
#create a dictionary
>>> h = {}
#add a key/value pair
>>> h['item'] = 'beer'
>>> h['count'] = 4
#interpolate using %d for int, %s for string
>>> s = 'I want %(count)d bottles of %(item)s' % h
>>> s
'I want 4 bottles of beer'
```

The next section shows you how to create an ordered dictionary.

ORDERED DICTIONARIES

Regular Python dictionaries iterate over key/value pairs in arbitrary order. Python 2.7 introduced a new OrderedDict class in the collections module. The OrderedDict API provides the same interface as regular dictionaries, but iterates over keys and values in a guaranteed order depending on when a key was first inserted:

```
>>> from collections import OrderedDict
>>> d = OrderedDict([('first', 1),
...                  ('second', 2),
...                  ('third', 3)])
>>> d.items()
[('first', 1), ('second', 2), ('third', 3)]
```

If a new entry overwrites an existing entry, the original insertion position is left unchanged:

```
>>> d['second'] = 4
>>> d.items()
[('first', 1), ('second', 4), ('third', 3)]
```

Deleting an entry and reinserting it will move it to the end:

```
>>> del d['second']
>>> d['second'] = 5
>>> d.items()
[('first', 1), ('third', 3), ('second', 5)]
```

Sorting Dictionaries

Python allows you to print the entries in a dictionary. For example, you can modify the code in the preceding section to display the alphabetically sorted words and their associated word count.

Python Multi-Dictionaries

You can define entries in a dictionary so that they reference lists or other types of structures. Listing 9.4 displays the content of `multi_dictionary1.py` that illustrates how to define more complex dictionaries.

LISTING 9.4: multi_dictionary1.py

```
from collections import defaultdict

d = {'a' : [1, 2, 3], 'b' : [4, 5]}
print('firsts:',d)

d = defaultdict(list)
d['a'].append(1)
d['a'].append(2)
d['b'].append(4)
print('second:',d)

d = defaultdict(set)
d['a'].add(1)
d['a'].add(2)
d['b'].add(4)
print('third:',d)
```

Listing 9.4 starts by defining the dictionary d and printing its contents. The next portion of Listing 9.4 specifies a list-oriented dictionary, and then modifies the values for the keys a and b. The final portion of Listing 9.4 specifies a set-oriented dictionary, and then modifies the values for the keys a and b as well. The output from Listing 9.4 is here:

```
first: {'a': [1, 2, 3], 'b': [4, 5]}
second: defaultdict(<type 'list'>, {'a': [1, 2], 'b': [4]})
third: defaultdict(<type 'set'>, {'a': set([1, 2]), 'b': set([4])})
```

LIST COMPREHENSIONS

Earlier, you were introduced to lists, along with various operations that you can perform on lists.

Listing 9.1 shows you various ways in which you can process the contents of a list that consists of strings.

LISTING 9.1: uppercase1.py

```
list1 = ['a', 'list', 'of', 'words']
list2 = [s.upper() for s in list1]
list3 = [s for s in list1 if len(s) <=2]
list4 = [s for s in list1 if 'w' in s]

print('list1:',list1)
print('list2:',list2)
print('list3:',list3)
print('list4:',list4)
```

Listing 9.1 starts by initializing the variable `list1` with a set of words, followed by the variable `list2` that is a list comprehension that converts the words in `list1` to their uppercase counterparts.

Next, the variable `list3` is a list comprehension that selects the words from `list1` that have length at most 2. Finally, the variable `list4` is another list comprehension that consists of the words in `list1` that contain the letter "w."

The next portion of Listing 9.1 consists of a block of `print()` statements that display the contents of these four variables. Launch the code in Listing 9.1, and you will see the following output:

```
list1: ['a', 'list', 'of', 'words']
list2: ['A', 'LIST', 'OF', 'WORDS']
list3: ['a', 'of']
list4: ['words']
```

Lists and Filter-related Operations

Python allows you to filter a list (also called *list comprehension*) as shown here:

```
mylist = [1, -2, 3, -5, 6, -7, 8]
pos = [n for n in mylist if n > 0]
neg = [n for n in mylist if n < 0]

print(pos)
print(neg)
```

You can also specify `if/else` logic in a filter, as shown here:

```
mylist = [1, -2, 3, -5, 6, -7, 8]
negativeList = [n if n < 0 else 0 for n in mylist]
positiveList = [n if n > 0 else 0 for n in mylist]

print(positiveList)
print(negativeList)
```

The output of the preceding code block is here:

```
[1, 3, 6, 8]
[-2, -5, -7]
[1, 0, 3, 0, 6, 0, 8]
[0, -2, 0, -5, 0, -7, 0]
```

Expressions in Lists

The following construct is similar to a `for` loop, but without the colon ":" character that appears at the end of a loop construct. Consider the following example:

```
nums = [1, 2, 3, 4]
cubes = [ n*n*n for n in nums ]

print('nums: ',nums)
print('cubes:',cubes)
```

The output from the preceding code block is here:

```
nums:   [1, 2, 3, 4]
cubes:  [1, 8, 27, 64]
```

SORTING LISTS OF NUMBERS AND STRINGS

Listing 9.2 displays the content of `sorted1.py` that determines whether two lists are sorted.

LISTING 9.2: sorted1.py

```
list1 = [1,2,3,4,5]
list2 = [2,1,3,4,5]

sort1 = sorted(list1)
sort2 = sorted(list2)

if(list1 == sort1):
  print(list1,'is sorted')
else:
  print(list1,'is not sorted')

if(list2 == sort2):
  print(list2,'is sorted')
else:
  print(list2,'is not sorted')
```

Listing 9.2 initializes the lists `list1` and `list2`, and the sorted lists `sort1` and `sort2` based on the lists `list1` and `list2`, respectively. If `list1` equals `sort1`, then `list1` is already sorted; similarly, if `list2` equals `sort2`, then `list2` is already sorted.

The output from Listing 9.2 is here:

```
[1, 2, 3, 4, 5] is sorted
[2, 1, 3, 4, 5] is not sorted
```

Note that if you sort a list of character strings the output is case sensitive, and that uppercase letters appear before lowercase letters. This is because the collating sequence for ASCII places uppercase letter (decimal 65 through decimal 91) before lowercase letters (decimal 97 through decimal 127). The following example provides an illustration:

```
>>> list1 = ['a', 'A', 'b', 'B', 'Z']
>>> print(sorted(list1))
['A', 'B', 'Z', 'a', 'b']
```

You can also specify the reverse option so that the list is sorted in reverse order:

```
>>> list1 = ['a', 'A', 'b', 'B', 'Z']
>>> print(sorted(list1, reverse=True))
['b', 'a', 'Z', 'B', 'A']
```

You can even sort a list based on the length of the items in the list:

```
>>> list1 = ['a', 'AA', 'bbb', 'BBBBB', 'ZZZZZZZ']
>>> print(sorted(list1, key=len))
['a', 'AA', 'bbb', 'BBBBB', 'ZZZZZZZ']
>>> print(sorted(list1, key=len, reverse=True))
['ZZZZZZZ', 'BBBBB', 'bbb', 'AA', 'a']
```

You can specify str.lower if you want treat uppercase letters as though they are lowercase letters during the sorting operation, as shown here:

```
>>> print(sorted(list1, key=str.lower))
['a', 'AA', 'bbb', 'BBBBB', 'ZZZZZZZ']
```

Lists and Arithmetic Operations

The minimum value of a list of numbers is the first number in the sorted list of numbers. If you reverse the sorted list, the first number is the maximum value. There are several ways to reverse a list, starting with the technique shown in the following code:

```
x = [3,1,2,4]
maxList = x.sort()
minList = x.sort(x.reverse())

min1 = min(x)
max1 = max(x)
print(min1)
print(max1)
```

The output of the preceding code block is here:

```
1
4
```

A second (and better) way to sort a list is shown here:

```
minList = x.sort(reverse=True)
```

A third way to sort a list involves the built-in functional version of the sort() method, as shown here:

```
sorted(x, reverse=True)
```

The preceding code snippet is useful when you do not want to modify the original order of the list or you want to compose multiple list operations on a single line.

CONCATENATING A LIST OF WORDS

Python provides the `join()` method for concatenating text strings, as shown here:

```
>>> parts = ['Is', 'SF', 'In', 'California?']
>>> ' '.join(parts)
'Is SF In California?'
>>> ','.join(parts)
'Is,SF,In,California?'
>>> ''.join(parts) 'IsSFInCalifornia?'
```

There are several ways to concatenate a set of strings and then print the result. The following is the most inefficient way to do so:

```
print("This" + " is" + " a" + " sentence")
```

Either of the following is preferred:

```
print("%s %s %s %s" % ("This", "is", "a", "sentence"))
print(" ".join(["This","is","a","sentence"]))
```

ARRAYS AND THE append() FUNCTION

Although Python does have an array type (`import array`), which is essentially a heterogeneous list, the array type has no advantages over the list type other than a slight savings in memory use.

You can define heterogeneous arrays as follows:

```
a = [10, 'hello', [5, '77']]
```

You can append a new element to an element inside a list:

```
>>> a = [10, 'hello', [5, '77']]
>>> a[2].append('abc')
>>> a
[10, 'hello', [5, '77', 'abc']]
```

You can assign simple variables to the elements of a list, as shown here:

```
myList = [ 'a', 'b', 91.1, (2014, 01, 31) ]
x1, x2, x3, x4 = myList
print('x1:',x1)
print('x2:',x2)
print('x3:',x3)
print('x4:',x4)
```

The output of the preceding code block is here:

```
x1: a
x2: b
x3: 91.1
x4: (2014, 1, 31)
```

The `split()` function is more convenient (especially when the number of elements is unknown or variable) than the preceding sample, and you will see examples of the `split()` function in the next section.

WORKING WITH LISTS AND THE split() FUNCTION

You can use the `split()` function to split the words in a text string and populate a list with those words. An example is here:

```
>>> x = "this is a string"
>>> list = x.split()
>>> list
['this', 'is', 'a', 'string']
```

A simple way to print the list of words in a text string is shown here:

```
>>> x = "this is a string"
>>> for w in x.split():
...     print(w)
...
this
is
a
string
```

You can search for a word in a string as follows:

```
>>> x = "this is a string"
>>> for w in x.split():
...     if(w == 'this'):
...         print("x contains this")
...
x contains this
...
```

COUNTING WORDS IN A LIST

Python provides the `Counter` class that enables you to count the words in a list. Listing 9.5 displays the content of `count_words2.py` that displays the top three words with greatest frequency.

LISTING 9.5: count_words2.py

```
from collections import Counter

mywords = ['a', 'b', 'a', 'b', 'c', 'a', 'd', 'e', 'f', 'b']
```

```
word_counts = Counter(mywords)
topThree = word_counts.most_common(3)
print(topThree)
```

Listing 9.5 initializes the variable `mywords` with a set of characters and then initializes the variable `word_counts` by passing `mywords` as an argument to `Counter`. The variable `topThree` is an array containing the three most common characters (and their frequency) that appear in `mywords`. The output from Listing 9.5 is here:

```
[('a', 3), ('b', 3), ('c', 1)]
```

ITERATING THROUGH PAIRS OF LISTS

Python supports operations on pairs of lists, which means that you can perform vector-like operations. The following snippet multiplies every list element by 3:

```
>>> list1 = [1, 2, 3]
>>> [3*x for x in list1]
[3, 6, 9]
```

Create a new list with pairs of elements consisting of the original element and the original element multiplied by 3 with the following code:

```
>>> list1 = [1, 2, 3]
>>> [[x, 3*x] for x in list1]
[[1, 3], [2, 6], [3, 9]]
```

Compute the product of every pair of numbers from two lists:

```
>>> list1 = [1, 2, 3]
>>> list2 = [5, 6, 7]
>>> [a*b for a in list1 for b in list2]
[5, 6, 7, 10, 12, 14, 15, 18, 21]
```

Calculate the sum of every pair of numbers from two lists:

```
>>> list1 = [1, 2, 3]
>>> list2 = [5, 6, 7]
>>> [a+b for a in list1 for b in list2]
[6, 7, 8, 7, 8, 9, 8, 9, 10]
```

Calculate the pair-wise product of two lists:

```
>>> [list1[i]*list2[i] for i in range(len(list1))]
[8, 12, -54]
```

OTHER LIST-RELATED FUNCTIONS

Python provides additional functions that you can use with lists, such as `append()`, `insert()`, `delete()`, `pop()`, and `extend()`. Python also supports the functions `index()`, `count()`, `sort()`, and `reverse()`. Examples of these functions are illustrated in the following code block.

Define a list (notice that duplicates are allowed):

```
>>> a = [1, 2, 3, 2, 4, 2, 5]
```

Display the number of occurrences of 1 and 2:

```
>>> print(a.count(1), a.count(2))
1 3
```

Insert -8 in position 3:

```
>>> a.insert(3,-8)
>>> a
[1, 2, 3, -8, 2, 4, 2, 5]
```

Remove occurrences of 3:

```
>>> a.remove(3)
>>> a
[1, 2, -8, 2, 4, 2, 5]
```

Remove occurrences of 1:

```
>>> a.remove(1)
>>> a
[2, -8, 2, 4, 2, 5]
```

Append 19 to the list:

```
>>> a.append(19)
>>> a
[2, -8, 2, 4, 2, 5, 19]
```

Print the index of 19 in the list:

```
>>> a.index(19)
6
```

Reverse the list:

```
>>> a.reverse()
>>> a
[19, 5, 2, 4, 2, -8, 2]
```

Sort the list:

```
>>> a.sort()
>>> a
[-8, 2, 2, 2, 4, 5, 19]
```

Extend list a with list b:

```
>>> b = [100,200,300]
>>> a.extend(b)
>>> a
[-8, 2, 2, 2, 4, 5, 19, 100, 200, 300]
```

Remove the first occurrence of 2:

```
>>> a.pop(2)
2
>>> a
[-8, 2, 2, 4, 5, 19, 100, 200, 300]
```

Remove the last item of the list:

```
>>> a.pop()
300
>>> a
[-8, 2, 2, 4, 5, 19, 100, 200]
```

NOTE *The "in" operator on a list to search is O(n), whereas the "in" operator on set is O(1).*

SUMMARY

This chapter showed you how to work with various Python data types. In particular, you learned about tuples, sets, and dictionaries. Next you learned how to work with lists and how to use list-related operations to extract sub-lists.

CHAPTER 10

INTRODUCTION TO RECURSION

This chapter introduces you to recursion through various Python code samples. Recursion is indispensable when working with algorithms that solve tasks involving trees and graphs, both of which are beyond the scope of this book. Recursive algorithms exist even for a simple data structures, such as an array of sorted elements; binary search is such an algorithm.

The first part of this chapter shows you how to calculate arithmetic series and geometric series using iterative algorithms, as well as recursive algorithms. These examples provide a gentler introduction to recursion if you are new to this topic (experienced users will move more quickly through these code samples). Next, you will learn about calculating factorial values of positive integers and Fibonacci numbers. Except for the iterative solution to Fibonacci numbers, these code samples do not involve data structures.

The second part of this chapter discusses concepts in combinatorics, such as permutations and combinations. Note that a thorough coverage of combinatorics can fill an entire undergraduate course in mathematics, whereas this chapter contains only some rudimentary concepts.

If you are new to recursion, be prepared to read the material more than once and practice working with the code samples, which will lead to a better understanding of recursion. However, you can also skip the material in this chapter until you encounter code samples later in this chapter that involve recursion.

WHAT IS RECURSION?

Recursion-based algorithms can provide elegant solutions to tasks that would be difficult to implement via iterative algorithms. For some tasks, such as calculating factorial values, the recursive solution and the iterative solution have comparable code complexity.

As a simple example, suppose that we want to add the integers from 1 to n (inclusive), and let n = 10 so that we have a concrete example. If we denote S as the partial sum of successively adding consecutive integers, then we have the following:

```
S = 1        // = 1
S = S + 2    // = 3
S = S + 3    // = 6
. . .
S = S + 10 // = 55
. . .
```

If we denote S(n) as the sum of the first n positive integers, then we have the following relationship:

```
S(1) = 1
S(n) = S(n-1) + n for n > 1
```

With the preceding observations in mind, the next section contains code samples for calculating the sum of the first n positive integers using an iterative approach and then with recursion.

ARITHMETIC SERIES

This section shows you how to calculate the sum of a set of positive integers, such as the numbers from 1 to n inclusive. The first algorithm uses an iterative approach, and the second algorithm uses recursion.

Before delving into the code samples, there is a simple way to calculate the closed form sum of the integers from 1 to n inclusive, which we will denote as S. Then, there are two ways to calculate S, as shown here:

```
S = 1 + 2     + 3     + . . . + (n-1) + n
S = n + (n-1) + (n-2) + . . . + 2     + 1
```

There are n columns on the right side of the preceding pair of equations, and each column has the sum equal to (n+1). Therefore, the sum of the right side of the equals sign is n*(n+1). Since the left side of the equals sign has the sum 2*S, we have the following result:

```
2*S = n*(n+1)
```

Now divide both sides by 2, and we get the well-known formula for the arithmetic sum of the first n positive integers:

```
S = n*(n+1)/2
```

Incidentally, the preceding formula was derived by a young student who was bored with performing the calculation manually: that student was Karl F. Gauss (who developed it in third grade).

Calculating Arithmetic Series (Iterative)

Listing 10.1 displays the content of arith_sum.py that illustrates how to calculate the sum of the numbers from 1 to n, inclusive, using an iterative approach.

LISTING 10.1: arith_sum.py

```
def arith_sum(n):
  sum = 0
  for i in range(1,n+1):
    sum += i
  return sum

max = 20
for j in range(2,max+1):
```

```
  sum = arith_sum(j)
  print("sum from 1 to",j,"=",sum)
```

Listing 10.1 starts with the function `arith_sum()`, which contains a loop that literately adds the numbers from 1 to n. The next portion of Listing 10.1 also contains a loop that iterates through the numbers from 2 to 20, inclusive, and then invokes `arith_sum()` with each value of the loop variable to calculate the sum of the integers from 1 to that value. Launch the code in Listing 10.1, and you will see the following output:

```
sum from 1 to 2 = 3
sum from 1 to 3 = 6
sum from 1 to 4 = 10
sum from 1 to 5 = 15
sum from 1 to 6 = 21
sum from 1 to 7 = 28
sum from 1 to 8 = 36
sum from 1 to 9 = 45
sum from 1 to 10 = 55
sum from 1 to 11 = 66
sum from 1 to 12 = 78
sum from 1 to 13 = 91
sum from 1 to 14 = 105
sum from 1 to 15 = 120
sum from 1 to 16 = 136
sum from 1 to 17 = 153
sum from 1 to 18 = 171
sum from 1 to 19 = 190
sum from 1 to 20 = 210
```

Modify the code in Listing 10.1 to calculate the sum of the squares, cubes, and fourth powers of the numbers from 1 to n, along with your own variations of the code.

Calculating Arithmetic Series (Recursive)

Listing 10.2 displays the content of `arith_sum_recursive.py` that illustrates how to calculate the sum of the numbers from 1 to n, inclusive, using a recursion.

LISTING 10.2: arith_sum_recursive.py

```
def arith_sum(n):
  if(n == 0):
    return n
  else:
    return n + arith_sum(n-1)

max = 20
for j in range(2,max+1):
  sum = arith_sum(j)
  print("sum from 1 to",j,"=",sum)
```

Listing 10.2 starts with the recursive function `arith_sum()`, which uses conditional logic to return n if n equals the value 0 (which is the terminating case); otherwise, the code returns the value of n *plus* the value of `arith_sum(n-1)`. Launch the code in Listing 10.2, and you will see the same output as the previous section.

Now that you have seen some examples involving arithmetic expressions, let's turn to geometric series, which is the topic of the next section.

GEOMETRIC SERIES

This section shows you how to calculate the geometric series of a set of positive integers, such as the numbers from 1 to n, inclusive. The first algorithm uses an iterative approach, and the second algorithm uses recursion.

Before delving into the code samples, there is a simple way to calculate the closed form sum of the geometric series of integers from 1 to n, inclusive, where r is the ratio of consecutive terms in the geometric series. Let S denote the sum, which we can express as follows:

```
S   = 1+ r + r^2 + r^3 + . . . + r^(n-1) + r^n
r*S =     r + r^2 + r^3 + . . . + r^(n-1) + r^n + r^(n+1)
```

Subtract each term in the second row above from the corresponding term in the first row, and we obtain the following result:

```
S - r*S = 1 - r^(n+1)
```

Factor s from both terms on the left side of the preceding equation, and we obtain the following result:

```
S*(1 - r) = 1 - r^(n+1)
```

Divide both sides of the preceding equation by the term `(1-r)` to obtain the formula for the sum of the geometric series of the first n positive integers:

```
2*S =
S = [1 - r^(n+1)]/(1-r)
```

If r = 1, then the preceding equation returns an infinite value, which makes sense because S is the sum of an infinite number of occurrences of the number 1.

Calculating a Geometric Series (Iterative)

Listing 10.3 displays the content of `geom_sum.py` that illustrates how to calculate the sum of the numbers from 1 to n, inclusive, using an iterative approach.

LISTING 10.3: geom_sum.py

```
def geom_sum(n,ratio):
  partial = 0
  power   = 1
  for i in range(1,n+1):
    partial += power
    power *= ratio
  return partial
```

```
max = 10
ratio = 2
for j in range(2,max+1):
  prod = geom_sum(j,ratio)
  print("geometric sum for ratio=",ratio,"from 1 to",j,"=",prod)
```

Listing 10.3 starts with the function geom_sum(), which contains a loop that calculates the sum of the powers of the numbers from 1 to n, where the power is the value of the variable ratio. The second part of Listing 10.3 contains a loop that invokes the function geom_sum() with the values 2, 3, . . ., n and a fixed value of 2 for the variable ratio. Launch the code in Listing 10.3, and you will see the following output:

```
geometric sum for ratio= 2 from 1 to 2 = 3
geometric sum for ratio= 2 from 1 to 3 = 7
geometric sum for ratio= 2 from 1 to 4 = 15
geometric sum for ratio= 2 from 1 to 5 = 31
geometric sum for ratio= 2 from 1 to 6 = 63
geometric sum for ratio= 2 from 1 to 7 = 127
geometric sum for ratio= 2 from 1 to 8 = 255
geometric sum for ratio= 2 from 1 to 9 = 511
geometric sum for ratio= 2 from 1 to 10 = 1023
```

Calculating Geometric Series (Recursive)

Listing 10.4 displays the content of geom_sum_recursive.py that illustrates how to calculate the sum of the geometric series of the numbers from 1 to n, inclusive, using recursion. Note that the following code sample uses *tail recursion*.

LISTING 10.4: geom_sum_recursive.py

```
def geom_sum(n,ratio,term,sum):
  if(n == 1):
    return sum
  else:
    term *= ratio
    sum += term
    return geom_sum(n-1,ratio,term,sum)

max = 10
ratio = 2
sum = 1
term = 1

for j in range(2,max+1):
  prod = geom_sum(j,ratio,term,sum)
  print("geometric sum for ratio=",ratio,"from 1 to",j,"=",prod)
```

Listing 10.4 contains the function geom_sum(), which takes four arguments: n (the current value of the upper range), ratio (which is the exponent 2 in this code sample), term (which is the current intermediate term of the sum), and sum (the target sum).

The code returns the value 1 when n equals 1; otherwise, the values of term and sum are updated, and the function geom_sum() is invoked whose *only* difference is to decrement n by 1.

This code sample illustrates tail recursion, which is more efficient than regular recursion, and perhaps a little more intuitive, as well. The second part of Listing 10.4 contains a loop that invokes the function geom_sum() as the loop iterates from 2 to max inclusive. Launch the code in Listing 10.4, and you will see the same output as the previous section.

FACTORIAL VALUES

This section contains three code samples for calculating factorial values: one code sample uses a loop and the other two code samples use recursion.

By way of introduction, the *factorial* value of a positive integer n is the product of all the numbers from 1 to n (inclusive). Hence, we have the following values:

```
Factorial(1)   = 1*1 = 1
Factorial(2)   = 2*1 = 2
Factorial(3)   = 3*2*1 = 6
Factorial(4)   = 4*3*2*1 = 24
Factorial(5)   = 5*4*3*2*1 = 120
Factorial(6)   = 6*5*4*3*2*1 = 720
Factorial(7)   = 7*6*5*4*3*2*1 = 5040
```

If you look at the preceding list of calculations, you can see some interesting relationships among factorial numbers:

```
Factorial(1)  = 1
Factorial(2)  = 2 * Factorial(1)
Factorial(3)  = 3 * Factorial(2)
Factorial(4)  = 4 * Factorial(3)
Factorial(5)  = 5 * Factorial(4)
Factorial(6)  = 6 * Factorial(5)
Factorial(7)  = 7 * Factorial(6)
```

Based on the preceding observations, it is reasonably intuitive to infer the following relationship for factorial numbers:

```
Factorial(1)  = 1
Factorial(n)  = n * Factorial(n-1) for n > 1
```

The next section uses the preceding formula to calculate the factorial value of various numbers.

Calculating Factorial Values (Iterative)

Listing 10.5 displays the content of Factorial1.py that illustrates how to calculate factorial numbers using an iterative approach.

LISTING 10.5: Factorial1.py

```
def factorial(n):
  prod = 1
  for i in range(1,n+1):
```

```
    prod *= i
  return prod

max = 20
for n in range(0,max):
  result = factorial(n)
  print("factorial",n,"=",result)
```

Listing 10.5 starts with the function `factorial()`, which contains a loop to multiply the numbers from 1 to n and stores the product in the variable `prod`, whose initial value is 1. The second part of Listing 10.5 contains a loop that invokes `factorial()` with the loop variable that ranges from 0 to `max`. Launch the code in Listing 10.5, and you will see the following output:

```
factorial 0 = 1
factorial 1 = 1
factorial 2 = 2
factorial 3 = 6
factorial 4 = 24
factorial 5 = 120
factorial 6 = 720
factorial 7 = 5040
factorial 8 = 40320
factorial 9 = 362880
factorial 10 = 3628800
factorial 11 = 39916800
factorial 12 = 479001600
factorial 13 = 6227020800
factorial 14 = 87178291200
factorial 15 = 1307674368000
factorial 16 = 20922789888000
factorial 17 = 355687428096000
factorial 18 = 6402373705728000
factorial 19 = 121645100408832000
```

Calculating Factorial Values (Recursive)

Listing 10.6 displays the content of `Factorial2.py` that illustrates how to calculate factorial values using recursion.

LISTING 10.6: Factorial2.py

```
def factorial(n):
  if(n <= 1):
    return 1
  else:
    return n * factorial(n-1)

max = 20
for n in range(0,max):
  result = factorial(n)
  print("factorial",n,"=",result)
```

Listing 10.6 starts with the function `factorial()`, which is the same function that you saw in Listing 10.5. Notice that the second portion of Listing 10.6 is the same as the second portion of Listing 10.5. Launch the code in Listing 10.6, and you will see the same output as the preceding example.

Calculating Factorial Values (Tail Recursion)

Listing 10.7 displays the content of `Factorial3.py` that illustrates how to calculate factorial values using tail recursion.

LISTING 10.7: Factorial3.py

```
def factorial(n, prod):
  if(n <= 1):
     return prod
  else:
     return factorial(n-1, n*prod)

max = 20
for n in range(0,max):
  result = factorial(n, 1)
print("factorial",n,"=",result)
```

Listing 10.7 starts with the recursive function `factorial()`, which uses tail recursion, and is somewhat analogous to the tail recursion in Listing 10.4. The second portion of Listing 10.7 is similar to the second portion of Listing 10.5: the difference involves the second argument that is the "base value" of the tail recursion, which in this case, equals 1. Launch the code in Listing 10.7, and you will see the same output as the preceding example.

FIBONACCI NUMBERS

Fibonacci numbers are simple and appear in nature (such as the pattern of sunflower seeds). The first two values of Fibonacci numbers are 0 and 1, respectively, and for any integer n >=2, the Fibonacci value of n is sum of the Fibonacci value of its two "predecessors," which are the Fibonacci of (n-1) plus the Fibonacci of (n-2). More concisely, here is the definition of the Fibonacci sequence:

```
Fib(0) = 0
Fib(1) = 1
Fib(n) = Fib(n-1)+Fib(n-2) for n >= 2
```

Note that it is possible to specify different "seed" values for `Fib(0)` and `Fib(1)`, but the values 0 and 1 are frequently used values.

Calculating Fibonacci Numbers (Recursive)

Listing 10.8 displays the content of `Fibonacci1.py` that illustrates how to calculate Fibonacci numbers using recursion.

LISTING 10.8: Fibonacci1.py

```
# very inefficient:
def fibonacci(n):
```

```
  if n <= 1:
    return n
  else:
    return fibonacci(n-2) + fibonacci(n-1)

max=20
for i in range(0,max):
  fib = fibonacci(i)
  print("fibonacci",i,"=",fib)
```

Listing 10.8 starts the recursive function `fibonacci()` that returns 1 if n equals 1. If n is greater than 1, the code returns the sum of *two* invocations of `fibonacci()`: the first with the value n-2 and the second with the value n-1.

The second part of Listing 10.8 contains another loop that invokes the function `fibonacci()` with the values of the loop variable that iterates from 0 to `max`. Launch the code in Listing 10.8, and you will see the following output:

```
fibonacci 0 = 0
fibonacci 1 = 1
fibonacci 2 = 1
fibonacci 3 = 2
fibonacci 4 = 3
fibonacci 5 = 5
fibonacci 6 = 8
fibonacci 7 = 13
fibonacci 8 = 21
fibonacci 9 = 34
fibonacci 10 = 55
fibonacci 11 = 89
fibonacci 12 = 144
fibonacci 13 = 233
fibonacci 14 = 377
fibonacci 15 = 610
fibonacci 16 = 987
fibonacci 17 = 1597
fibonacci 18 = 2584
fibonacci 19 = 4181
```

Calculating Fibonacci Numbers (Iterative)

Listing 10.9 displays the content of `Fibonacci2.py` that illustrates how to calculate Fibonacci numbers using an iterative approach.

LISTING 10.9: Fibonacci2.py

```
import numpy as np

max=20
arr1 = np.zeros(max)
arr1[0] = 0
arr1[1] = 1

for i in range(2,max):
  arr1[i] = arr1[i-1] + arr1[i-2]
  print("fibonacci",i,"=",arr1[i])
```

Listing 10.9 also calculates the values of Fibonacci numbers; however, this code sample stores intermediate values in an array. Despite the overhead of an array, this code is much more efficient than the code in Listing 10.8. Launch the code in Listing 10.9, and you will see the same output as the previous section.

TASK: REVERSE A STRING VIA RECURSION

Listing 10.10 displays the content of `reverser.py` that illustrates how to use recursion to reverse a string.

LISTING 10.10: reverser.py

```python
import numpy as np

def reverser(str):
   if(str == None or len(str) == 0):
      return str
   print("all-but-first chars:",str[1:])
   return reverser(str[1:])+list(str[0])

names = np.array(["Nancy", "Dave", "Dominic"])

for name in names:
   str_list = list(name)
   result = reverser(str_list)
   print("=> Word: ",name," reverse: ",result)
   print()
```

Listing 10.10 starts with the recursive function `reverser()` that invokes itself with a substring that omits the first character, which is appended to the result of invoking `reverser()` recursively, as shown here:

```python
return reverser(str[1:])+list(str[0])
```

The second part of Listing 10.10 contains a loop that invokes the `reverser()` method with different strings that belong to an array. Launch the code in Listing 10.10, and you will see the following output:

```
all-but-first chars: ['a', 'n', 'c', 'y']
all-but-first chars: ['n', 'c', 'y']
all-but-first chars: ['c', 'y']
all-but-first chars: ['y']
all-but-first chars: []
=> Word:  Nancy  reverse:  ['y', 'c', 'n', 'a', 'N']

all-but-first chars: ['a', 'v', 'e']
all-but-first chars: ['v', 'e']
all-but-first chars: ['e']
all-but-first chars: []
=> Word:  Dave  reverse:  ['e', 'v', 'a', 'D']
```

```
all-but-first chars: ['o', 'm', 'i', 'n', 'i', 'c']
all-but-first chars: ['m', 'i', 'n', 'i', 'c']
all-but-first chars: ['i', 'n', 'i', 'c']
all-but-first chars: ['n', 'i', 'c']
all-but-first chars: ['i', 'c']
all-but-first chars: ['c']
all-but-first chars: []
=> Word:  Dominic  reverse:  ['c', 'i', 'n', 'i', 'm', 'o', 'D']
```

TASK: CHECK FOR BALANCED PARENTHESES

This task involves only round parentheses: later, you will see an example of checking for balanced parentheses that can include square brackets and curly braces. Here are some examples of strings that contain round parentheses:

```
S1 = "()()()"
S2 = "(()()())"
S3 = "()("
S4 = "(())"
S5 = "()()("
```

The strings S, S3, and S4 have balanced parentheses, whereas the strings S2 and S5 have unbalanced parentheses.

Listing 10.11 displays the content of balanced_parens.py that illustrates how to determine whether a string consists of balanced parentheses.

LISTING 10.11: balanced_parens.py

```python
import numpy as np

def check_balanced(text):
  counter = 0
  text_len = len(text)

  for i in range(text_len):
    if (text[i] == '('):
      counter += 1
    else:
      if (text[i] == ')'):
        counter -= 1

    if (counter < 0):
      break

  if (counter == 0):
    print("balanced string:",text)
  else:
    print("unbalanced string:",text)
  print()

exprs = np.array(["()()()", "(()()())","()(","(())","()()("])

for str in exprs:
  check_balanced(str)
```

Listing 10.11 starts with the iterative function `check_balanced()`, which uses conditional logic to check the contents of the current character in the input string. The code increments the variable `counter` if the current character is a left parenthesis "(," and decrements the variable `counter` if the current character is a right parenthesis ")." The only way for an expression to consist of a balanced set of parentheses is for counter to equal 0 when the loop has finished execution.

The second part of Listing 10.11 contains a loop that invokes the function `check_balanced()` with different strings that are part of an array of strings. Launch the code in Listing 10.11, and you will see the following output:

```
exprs = np.array(["()()()", "(()()())","()(","(())","()()("])
balanced string: ()()()

balanced string: (()()())

unbalanced string: ()(

balanced string: (())

unbalanced string: ()()(
```

TASK: DETERMINE IF A POSITIVE INTEGER IS PRIME

Listing 10.12 displays the content of `check_prime.py` that illustrates how to calculate the number of digits in positive integers.

LISTING 10.12: check_prime.py

```python
import numpy as np

PRIME = 1
COMPOSITE = 0

def is_prime(num):
  div = 2

  while(div*div < num):
   if( num % div != 0):
      div += 1
   else:
      return COMPOSITE
  return PRIME


upperBound = 20

for num in range(2, upperBound):
  result = is_prime(num)
  if(result == True):
    print(num,": is prime")
  else:
    print(num,": is not prime")
```

Listing 10.12 starts with the function is_prime(), which contains a loop that checks whether any integer in the range of 2 to sqrt(num) divides the parameter num, and then returns the appropriate result.

The second portion of Listing 10.12 contains a loop that iterates through the numbers from 2 to upperBound (which has the value 20) to determine which numbers are prime. Launch the code in Listing 10.12, and you will see the following output:

```
2 : is prime
3 : is prime
4 : is not prime
5 : is prime
6 : is not prime
7 : is prime
8 : is not prime
9 : is not prime
10 : is not prime
11 : is prime
12 : is not prime
13 : is prime
14 : is not prime
15 : is not prime
16 : is not prime
17 : is prime
18 : is not prime
19 : is prime
```

SUMMARY

This chapter started with an introduction to recursion, along with various code samples that involve calculating the sum of an arithmetic series and the sum of a geometric series. In addition, you saw how to calculate factorial values and Fibonacci numbers.

Miscellaneous Topics

This chapter contains an assortment of topics, such as functionally-oriented programming, generators and iterators, and magic methods ("dunders").

The first part of this chapter discusses functional programming, which includes iterators such as filter(), map(), and reduce(), which enable you to iterate over the items in a data structure.

The second part of this chapter discusses lambda expressions, along with some code samples that illustrate how to define them.

The third section describes the concept of a pipe, after which you will learn about generators. The last section contains various code samples involving generators, such as generating a list of prime numbers.

FUNCTIONALLY-ORIENTED PROGRAMMING

Python 3 supports *iterators*, such as filter(), map(), and reduce(), which are useful when you need to iterate over the items in a list, create a dictionary, or extract a subset of a list. These iterators are discussed in the following subsections.

The filter() Function

The filter() function allows you to extract a subset of values based on conditional logic. The following example returns a list of odd numbers between 0 and 15, inclusive, that are multiples of 3:

```
>>> range(0,15)
[0, 1, 2, 3, 4, 5, 6, 7, 8, 9, 10, 11, 12, 13, 14]
>>> def f(x): return x % 2 != 0 and x % 3 == 0
...
>>> filter(f, range(0, 15))
[3, 9]
>>>
```

The map() Function

The map() function is a built-in function that applies a function to each item in an iterable. The map(func, seq) calls func(item), where item is an element in a sequence seq, and returns a list of the return values.

Listing 11.1 displays the content of map1.py that illustrates how to use the map() function to compute the cube and fourth power of a set of numbers.

LISTING 11.1: map1.py

```
def cube(x): return x*x*x
def fourth(x): return x*x*x*x

x1 = map(cube,   range(1, 5))
x2 = map(fourth, range(1, 5))

print(x1)
print(x2)
```

Listing 11.1 starts with the definition of two functions called cube() and fourth(), each of which takes a single numeric value. The cube() function returns the cube of its argument, and the fourth() function returns the fourth power of its argument.

The next portion of Listing 11.1 contains two invocations of the map() function. The first invocation specifies the cube() function as the first parameter, and the integers between 1 and 4 inclusive as the second parameter via the range() function. The second invocation specifies the fourth() function as the first parameter, along with the integers between 1 and 4 inclusive. The output from Listing 11.1 is here:

```
[1, 8, 27, 64]
[1, 16, 81, 256]
```

The reduce() Function

The reduce(func, seq) function returns a single value constructed by calling the binary function func on the first two items of the sequence seq to compute a result, and then applies func on that result and the *next* item in seq, and so on until a single value is returned. Thus, the reduce() function repeatedly performs a pair-wise reduction (and hence its name) on a sequence until a single value is computed.

In case the functionality of the reduce() function is new to you, there are other scenarios that have similar functionality. For example, recall that multiplication of two numbers is implemented as repeated addition (along with a shift operator).

THE LAMBDA OPERATOR AND LAMBDA EXPRESSIONS

The lambda operator (or *lambda function*) allows you to define "anonymous" functions that are often used in combination with the functions filter(), map(), and reduce().

An example of a lambda function that adds two arguments is here:

```
>>> f = lambda x,y : x + y
>>> f(2,3)
5
```

You can also combine lambda functions with the `reduce()` function. For example, the following code snippet defines a lambda function `f` to add a pair of numbers, along with invoking the `reduce()` function that applies the lambda function `f` to a sequence `range(1,6)` to calculate the sum of the numbers 1 through 6:

```
>>> f = lambda x,y: x+y
>>> reduce(f, range(1,6))
15
```

Lambda Expressions

Listing 11.2 displays the content of `lambda1.py` that illustrates how to create a simple lambda function.

LISTING 11.2: lambda1.py

```
add = lambda x, y: x + y

x1 = add(5,7)
x2 = add('Hello', 'Python')

print(x1)
print(x2)
```

Listing 11.2 defines the lambda expression `add` that accepts two input parameters and then returns their sum (for numbers) or their concatenation (for strings). The output from Listing 11.2 is here:

```
12
HelloPython
```

The following example shows you how to assign values to variables from a more complex data structure:

```
>>> line = ['a', 10, 20, (2024,01,31)]
>>> x1,x2,x3,date1 = line
>>> x1
'a'
>>> x2
10
>>> x3
20
>>> date1
(2024, 1, 31)
```

If you want to access the year/month/date components of the `date1` element in the preceding code block, you can do so with the following code block:

```
>>> line = ['a', 10, 20, (2024,01,31)]
>>> x1,x2,x3,(year,month,day) = line
>>> x1
'a'
>>> x2
```

```
10
>>> x3
20
>>> year
2024
>>> month
1
>>> day
31
```

If the number and/or structure of the variables do not match the data, an error message is displayed, as shown here:

```
>>> point = (1,2)
>>> x,y,z = point
Traceback (most recent call last):
  File "<stdin>", line 1, in <module>
ValueError: need more than 2 values to unpack
```

If the number of variables that you specify is less than the number of data items, you will see an error message, as shown here:

```
>>> line = ['a', 10, 20, (2014,01,31)]
>>> x1,x2 = line
Traceback (most recent call last):
  File "<stdin>", line 1, in <module>
ValueError: too many values to unpack
```

DUNDERS AND MAGIC METHODS

This section contains a very brief description of "dunder" methods (shortened from "Double Underscores"). Such methods are also called *magic methods*. Magic methods can classified in terms of their functionality. For example, the first subset of the following magic methods overrides various Boolean operators, and the second subset override binary arithmetic operators:

- __le__()
- __lt__()
- __ge__()
- __gt__()
- __add__()
- __sub__()
- __mul__()
- __div__()

In addition, `Python` supports magic methods for handling tasks such as iteration and displaying the properties of an object or data structure, some of which are shown here:

- __iter__()
- __len__()
- __repr__()
- __str__()

In addition to the preceding list of magic methods, there are some associated functions that are typically invoked instead of (or in conjunction with) the methods in the preceding list, as shown here:

- `iter()`
- `len()`
- `repr()`
- `str()`

An extensive list of `Python` magic methods is available online:

https://www.geeksforgeeks.org/dunder-magic-methods-python/

https://stackoverflow.com/questions/56238263/list-of-all-python-dunder-magic-methods-which-ones-do-you-need-to-implement-to

The Iterator Protocol

The *iterator protocol* is a mechanism that enables you to iterate through container objects. Specifically, a container object (such as an instance of a custom class) must define the method `container.__iter__()` to support iteration for a container object. Moreover, the method `container.__iter__()` returns an `iterator` object, which in turn must support the following pair of methods that constitute the iterator protocol:

```
iterator.__iter__()
iterator.__next__()
```

The preceding pair of methods serve different purposes. The first method `iterator.__iter__()` returns the iterator object itself so that containers and iterators can be used with various statements, such as `for` statements and `in` statements. The second method, `iterator.__next__()`, is the method that returns the next item from the container. As mentioned earlier, Python iterators are available for comprehensions, loop constructs, and other built-in functions, including `map()`, `filter()`, `reduce()`, and `zip()`.

The next section discusses the `iter()` function and the `__iter__()` method and how they work together.

The iter() Function and the __iter__() Method

The `iter()` function is a Python built-in function that returns an iterator of a given object, an example of which is here:

```
iter(object)
```

Keep in mind that the `iter()` function requires an argument that is either an *iterable* or a *sequence*. In general, the `object` argument can be *any* object that supports either iteration or sequence protocol.

When you invoke the `iter()` function on an object, the function first searches for the presence of an `__iter__()` method of that object. If the `__iter__()` method exists, the `iter()` function calls that method to get an iterator.

If the __iter__() method does not exist, then the iter() function will search for a __getitem__() method. If the __getitem__() exists, the iter() function creates an iterator object and returns that object. If the __getitem__() does not exist, a TypeError exception is raised.

You also have the option to invoke either the iter() function or the __iter__() method to achieve the same result, with one important difference. The iter() function performs some additional type checking to determine whether the __iter__() method returns an iterator object. If an iterator object is not returned, then iter() throws an error. This same functionality is performed in the pair next() and __next__().

The methods __iter__() and __next__() are user-defined methods for ensuring that a custom class is meant to be an iterator. Note that an iterator cannot be reused after all items have been "iterated."

For instance, a list is an ordered collection of items that is also an iterable because a list object has the __iter__() method that returns an iterator. Here is an example:

```
numbers = [1, 2, 3]
number_iterator = numbers.__iter__()
print(type(number_iterator))
```

The preceding code block generates the following output:

```
<class 'list_iterator'>
```

Dictionaries and Iterators

The operators .keys(), .values(), and .items() provide iterators for the list of keys, values, and items, respectively, of a dictionary. Consequently, any modification of a dictionary results in a corresponding change in the iterators. Here is an example:

```
mydict = {'Dave': 35, 'Sara': 28}
mykeys = mydict.keys()
mydict['Peter'] = 40
for key in mykeys:
    print(key)
```

The output of the preceding code block is here:

```
Dave
Sara
Peter
```

If we want to iterate through a dictionary that *ignores* subsequent modifications to the dictionary, we can do so by constructing a list from the dictionary, as shown here:

```
mydict = {'Dave': 35, 'Sara': 28}
mylist = list(mydict.keys())
mykeys = mydict.keys()
mydict['Peter'] = 40

for item in mylist:
  print("item:",item)
```

```
for key in mykeys:
  print("key:",key)
```

The output of the preceding code block is here:

```
Dave
Sara
```

As you can see, the contents of `mylist` are "decoupled" from `mydict`, and therefore modifications to `mydict` are not reflected in `mylist`.

EXAMPLES OF ITERATORS

The `range()` function is an iterator, and it has the ability to generate a sequence of integers when it is invoked. Thus, the `range()` function must be invoked to generate a list of values. A list occupies actual memory locations. Specifically, the code snippet `range(10000)` *does not* generate 10,000 numbers unless this function is invoked, an example of which is shown here:

```
for num in range(10):
  print("num:",num)
```

The following code snippet contains a list of integers that *does* occupy memory locations:

```
my_list = [1,2,3,4,5,6,7,8,9,10]
```

The preceding distinction between a list and the `range()` function is important because there are situations where you would needlessly generate values that are not processed.

For example, suppose that the function `one_million()` returns the first one million integers. The function `add_three()` invokes the method `one_million()`, and then calculates the sum of the first three integers and ignores the remaining 999,997 numbers. This type of code is extremely inefficient (and also unlikely, of course).

Instead of generating an entire set of numbers, a better approach is to generate and process only the numbers that are required. This approach is achievable by defining generators, which are described later in this chapter.

Range Versus a List

We can use the `range()` function to iterate through a sequence of numbers, as shown here:

```
for num in range(10):
  print("num: ", num)
```

The output from the preceding code snippet is here:

```
num:   0
num:   1
num:   2
num:   3
num:   4
num:   5
num:   6
```

```
num:    7
num:    8
num:    9
```

We can also create a list of values from the `range()` function, as shown here:

```
x = list(range(10))
print(x)
```

The output from the preceding code snippet is here:

```
[0, 1, 2, 3, 4, 5, 6, 7, 8, 9]
```

As you can see, when you invoke the `list()` function as a "wrapper" around the `range()` method, the result is a list of values. Hence, a `list` is different from the `range()` function. Moreover, we can find the type of the `range()` function with this code snippet:

```
x = range(10)
print(type(x))
```

In essence, you can think of the `range()` function as a function you can call repeatedly to obtain successive values from an underlying sequence of numbers, thereby eliminating the need to store a list of numbers. As an example, the following code snippet initializes the variable x with a list of 100 numbers, and therefore requires memory allocation:

```
x = list(range(100))
print(x)
```

By contrast, the following code snippet does not create a list or allocate memory:

```
x = range(100)
print(x)
```

The following code block requires memory only for the variables i and j:

```
j = 0
for i in range(100):
  j += i

print(j)
```

However, the following code block requires memory for i, j, *and* the list of 100 integers:

```
j = 0
for i in list(range(100)):
  j += i
print(j)
```

WHAT IS A PIPE?

A *pipe* is a logical concept, which is to say it is not physical object. By way of illustration, consider the following scenario:

- Person A stands inside a truck and gives boxes to person B outside the truck.
- Person A can only provide one box at a time.
- Person B can only move one box at a time (in this example, to the backyard).

The preceding scenario can be described as a producer/consumer or as a writer/reader:

- The producer puts "stuff" in the pipe, and the consumer reads that "stuff."
- If the pipe is full, the producer waits for the consumer to read "stuff"
- If the pipe is empty, the consumer waits for the producer to put "stuff" in the pipe.

One variation of the preceding scenario includes the writer placing a single item in the pipe and then waits until the reader removes the item from the pipe. Another variation involves writing to a pipe and reading from a pipe at both "ends" of the pipe.

With the preceding concepts in mind, you are in a position to understand how Python generators work, which is the topic of the next section.

WORKING WITH GENERATORS

A *generator function* allows you to pause a function and then resume the function later by means of the `yield` statement. An example of a generator is the `range()` function, but not the `list()` function. You can think of a generator function as a "producer," and the code that invoked the generator function is the "consumer." Hence, the consumer uses a pull-based mechanism to obtain values from the producer. Moreover, a generator produces values until it is completed or the `yield` statement is encountered, which is discussed in the next section.

Please read the following articles:

https://realpython.com/introduction-to-python-generators/

https://www.pythontutorial.net/advanced-python/python-generators/

The yield Keyword

Let's consider what happens when a `return` statement appears in the body of a function: the function is exited, and the state of any variables in that function is not retained.

By contrast, a generator function does retain state. Specifically, the `yield` keyword "emits" a value to the "calling" code, and then pauses the execution of the generator function. The next time that the calling code invokes the generator function, the code in that generator functions resumes at the location of the `yield` keyword. By way of analogy, the `yield` keyword acts like a writer to a pipe: the writer writes ("emits") a value to the pipe, and then pauses execution. When the reader reads the value in the pipe, the writer writes ("emits") another value to the pipe.

To illustrate the functionality of the `yield` keyword, Listing 11.3 displays the content of `yield1.py` that illustrates how to use the `yield keyword` to generate a list of integers.

LISTING 11.3: yield1.py

```
def make_numbers(m):
  i = 0
  while i < m:
```

```
      yield i
      i += 1

for i in make_numbers(10):
   print("i is now", i)

x = make_numbers(5)
print(type(x))
```

Listing 11.3 starts with the definition of the custom Python generator `make_numbers()`, which contains a loop with a `yield` statement that "emits" the current value of the variable `i` (which is initialized as 0) to the `for` statement that invokes this generator.

The next portion of Listing 11.3 is a loop that invokes the `make_numbers()` generator 10 times, followed by a code snippet that initializes the variable `x` and displays its type. Launch the code in Listing 11.3, and you will see the following output:

```
i is now 0
i is now 1
i is now 2
i is now 3
i is now 4
i is now 5
i is now 6
i is now 7
i is now 8
i is now 9
```

Generators and Comprehensions

The previous section showed you how to define a Python generator, and this section contains an example of one. As a reminder, the following code snippet is an example of a list comprehension that generates the squares of the integers between 0 and 9 inclusive:

```
x = [i**2 for i in range(10)]
```

Replace the square brackets with parentheses in the preceding comprehension to define a generator comprehension:

```
y = (i**2 for i in range(10))
print(y)
```

The next code block shows you how to define a Python generator in conjunction with the `sum()` function to calculate the sum of the squares of the integers between 0 and 99 inclusive:

```
def square_numbers(m):
    i = 0
    while i < m:
        yield i**2
        i += 1

x = sum(square_numbers(100))
print(f"Sum of the first hundred square numbers {x}")
```

The output of the preceding code block is shown here:

```
Sum of the first hundred square numbers 328350
```

A Generator Without a Loop

Listing 11.4 displays the content of `simple_gen.py` that illustrates how to "step" through different portions of code in a custom Python generator.

LISTING 11.4: simple_gen.py

```
def simple_gen():
  print("First time")
  yield 1
  print("Second time")
  yield 2
  print("Third time")
  yield 3

result = simple_gen()
#print("result:",result)
print("result:",next(result))
print("result:",next(result))
print("result:",next(result))
print("---------\n")

print("=> for loop:")
result = simple_gen()
for ndx in range(0,3):
  print("result:",next(result))
```

Listing 11.4 contains a generator that yields three integers 1, 2, and 3 during each invocation of this generator. The three invocations occur in the middle portion of Listing 11.4. The next portion of Listing 11.4 initializes the variable `result`, which is a generator object.

The final portion of Listing 11.4 contains a loop that invokes `next(result)` to invoke the generator. When `next()` is invoked, Python will invoke the `__next__()` method on the function that you pass in as a parameter. Launch the code in Listing 11.4, and you will see the following output:

```
First time
result: 1
Second time
result: 2
Third time
result: 3
---------

=> for loop:
First time
result: 1
Second time
result: 2
Third time
result: 3
```

MISCELLANEOUS EXAMPLES OF GENERATORS

The following subsections contain an assortment of code samples that are also generators. You will see examples of generating the squares of numbers, generating an infinite list of integers, and finding prime numbers.

Generate Squares of Numbers

Listing 11.5 displays the content of `gen_squares.py` that illustrates how to use the `yield` keyword to generate the squares of numbers.

LISTING 11.5: gen_squares.py

```
def square_numbers(m):
  i = 0
  while i < m:
    yield i**2
    i += 1

max = 5
print("=> squares of integers:")
for value in square_numbers(max):
  print("value:",value)

print("=> sum of squares:")
the_sum = sum(square_numbers(max))
print(f"Sum of squared integers: {the_sum}")

# invoke the next() built-in function
# to execute the body of the function:
print("=> single invocation:")
answer = square_numbers(5)
print("answer:",answer)
print("answer:",next(answer))
```

Listing 11.5 starts with the definition of the generator `square_numbers()` that contains a loop with a `yield` statement that "emits" the square of the variable i that is initialized with the value 0. The next portion of Listing 11.5 contains a loop that invokes the `square_numbers()` generator and then prints the value that is "emitted" by this generator.

The next portion of Listing 11.5 initializes the variable `the_sum` with the sum of the squared values that are returned by the generator `square_numbers()`. The final portion of Listing 11.5 initializes the variable `answer` with the result of invoking `square_numbers(5)`. In addition, the values of `answer` and `next(answer)` are displayed. Launch the code in Listing 11.5, and you will see the following output:

```
=> squares of integers:
value: 0
value: 1
value: 4
value: 9
value: 16
=> sum of squares:
```

```
Sum of squared integers: 30
=> single invocation:
answer: <generator object square_numbers at 0x10094d040>
answer: 0
```

Generate an Infinite List of Integers

Listing 11.6 displays the content of `primes1.py` that illustrates how to use the `yield` keyword to generate an infinite list of integers.

LISTING 11.6: gen_infinite.py

```
def infinite_integers():
  num = 0
  while True:
    yield num
    num += 1

max_value = 20
for num in infinite_integers():
  print("num:",num)
  # removing the 'if' statement
  # generates an infinite list:
  if(num > max_value):
    break
```

Listing 11.6 defines the generator function `infinite_integers()` that initializes the variable `num` with 0, and then enters a loop. The loop consists of two code snippets involving a yield statement and a code snippet to increment the value of the variable `num`. Notice there is no conditional logic for exiting the loop: this logic is part of the loop that invokes the function `infinite_integers()`.

The next portion of Listing 11.6 contains a loop that invokes `infinite_integers()` and prints the value "emitted" by the generator function. The other portion of the loop is conditional logic that exits the loop when the value of `num` exceeds the variable `max_value` (initialized as 20). Launch the code in Listing 11.6, and you will see the following output:

```
num: 0
num: 1
num: 2
num: 3
num: 4
num: 5
num: 6
num: 7
num: 8
num: 9
num: 10
num: 11
num: 12
num: 13
num: 14
num: 15
num: 16
```

```
num: 17
num: 18
num: 19
num: 20
num: 21
```

Find Prime Numbers

Listing 11.7 displays the content of `primes1.py` that illustrates how to use the `yield` keyword to determine the prime numbers in a list of integers.

LISTING 11.7: primes1.py

```
def primeNumbers(n):
  if n < 2: return
  numbers = list(range(2, n+1))
  print("entering while loop:")

  while numbers:
    prime = numbers[0]
    #print("prime:",prime)
    yield prime

    numbers = [num for num in numbers if num % prime !=0]
    print("numbers:",numbers)

for num in primeNumbers(30):
    print("=> generator returned prime:",num)
```

Listing 11.7 starts with the function `primes()` that finds prime numbers in the range of 2 and n, where n is initialized with the value 30 (later in the code). In addition, this function initializes the variable `numbers`, which is a list of numbers in the range 2 through n inclusive.

Next, this function contains a loop that processes the variable `prime`, which is first element in the variable `numbers`. The next code snippet in the loop is a yield statement that "emits" the current value of variable `prime`. Let's examine what happens when the value of `prime` is "emitted," which is described in the next paragraph.

The second portion of Listing 11.7 is a `for` loop that invokes the generator function `primeNumbers()`, which receives the value "emitted" by the `yield` statement in the generator function `primeNumbers()`. After the "emitted" value is printed, the loop invokes the function `primeNumbers()` again, at which point the function regenerates a comprehension of integers, as shown here:

```
numbers = [num for num in numbers if num % prime !=0]
```

The result of regenerating the comprehension numbers is that only prime numbers will be printed. Launch the code in Listing 11.7, and you will see the following output:

```
entering while loop:
=> generator returned prime: 2
numbers: [3, 5, 7, 9, 11, 13, 15, 17, 19, 21, 23, 25, 27, 29]
=> generator returned prime: 3
```

```
numbers: [5, 7, 11, 13, 17, 19, 23, 25, 29]
=> generator returned prime: 5
numbers: [7, 11, 13, 17, 19, 23, 29]
=> generator returned prime: 7
numbers: [11, 13, 17, 19, 23, 29]
=> generator returned prime: 11
numbers: [13, 17, 19, 23, 29]
=> generator returned prime: 13
numbers: [17, 19, 23, 29]
=> generator returned prime: 17
numbers: [19, 23, 29]
=> generator returned prime: 19
numbers: [23, 29]
=> generator returned prime: 23
numbers: [29]
=> generator returned prime: 29
numbers: []
```

Incidentally, Listing 11.7 is an implementation of the Sieve of Eratosthenes, which is one of the oldest algorithms for finding prime numbers.

SUMMARY

This chapter started with an explanation of functional programming in Python, which includes iterators such as filter(), map(), and reduce() that enable you to iterate over the items in a data structure. Next, you learned about lambda expressions, along with some code samples that illustrate how to define lambda expressions.

In addition, you learned about the concept of a pipe, which enabled you to understand the concept of generators. Finally, you saw various code samples involving generators, such as generating a list of prime numbers.

INTRODUCTION TO NUMPY

This appendix provides a quick introduction to the Python NumPy package, which provides a useful functionality, not only for "regular" Python scripts, but also for Python-based scripts with TensorFlow. For instance, this appendix contains NumPy code samples containing loops, arrays, and lists. We also discuss dot products, the `reshape()` method, how to plot with Matplotlib, and examples of linear regression.

The first part of this appendix briefly discusses NumPy and some of its useful features. The second part contains examples of working arrays in NumPy, and contrasts some of the APIs for lists with the same APIs for arrays. In addition, we show how to compute the exponent-related values (such as the square or cube) of elements in an array.

The second part of the appendix introduces sub-ranges, which are useful (and frequently used) for extracting portions of datasets in machine learning tasks. Some of the code samples handle negative (−1) sub-ranges for vectors and arrays because they are interpreted one way for vectors and in a different way for arrays.

The third part of this appendix delves into other NumPy methods, including the `reshape()` method, which useful when working with image files. Some TensorFlow APIs require converting a 2D array of (R, G, B) values into a corresponding one-dimensional vector.

WHAT IS NUMPY?

NumPy is a Python library that contains many convenient methods and aids with program performance. NumPy provides a core library for scientific computing in Python, with performant multi-dimensional arrays and good vectorized math functions, along with support for linear algebra and random numbers.

NumPy is modeled after MATLAB, with support for lists, arrays, and so forth. NumPy is easier to use than MATLAB, and it is very common in TensorFlow code as well as Python code.

Useful NumPy Features

The NumPy package provides the `ndarray` object that encapsulates multi-dimensional arrays of homogeneous data types. Many `ndarray` operations are performed in compiled code to improve performance.

There are important differences between NumPy arrays and the standard Python sequences. First, NumPy arrays have a fixed size, whereas Python lists can expand dynamically. Second, NumPy arrays are homogeneous, which means that the elements in a NumPy array must have the same data type. Third, NumPy arrays support more efficient execution (and require less code) of various types of operations on large numbers of data.

WHAT ARE NUMPY ARRAYS?

An *array* is a set of consecutive memory locations used to store data. Each item in the array is called an *element*. The number of elements in an array is called the *dimension* of the array. A typical array declaration is as follows:

```
arr1 = np.array([1,2,3,4,5])
```

The preceding code snippet declares `arr1` as an array of five elements, which you can access via `arr1[0]` through `arr1[4]`. Notice that the first element has an index value of 0, and the second element has an index value of 1. Thus, if you declare an array of 100 elements, then the 100th element has index value of 99.

NOTE   *The first position in a NumPy array has an index of 0.*

NumPy treats arrays as vectors. Math operations are performed element-by-element. Remember the following difference: "doubling" an array multiplies each element by 2, whereas "doubling" a list appends a list to itself.

Listing A.1 shows the content of `nparray1.py` that illustrate some operations on a NumPy array.

LISTING A.1: nparray1.py

```
import numpy as np

list1 = [1,2,3,4,5]
print(list1)

arr1  = np.array([1,2,3,4,5])
print(arr1)

list2 = [(1,2,3),(4,5,6)]
print(list2)

arr2  = np.array([(1,2,3),(4,5,6)])
print(arr2)
```

Listing A.1 defines the variables `list1` and `list2` (which are Python lists), as well as the variables `arr1` and `arr2` (which are arrays), and prints their values. The output from launching Listing A.1 is as follows:

```
[1, 2, 3, 4, 5]
[1 2 3 4 5]
[(1, 2, 3), (4, 5, 6)]
[[1 2 3]
 [4 5 6]]
```

WORKING WITH LOOPS

Listing A.2 shows the content of `loop1.py`, which illustrates how to iterate through the elements of a NumPy array and a Python list.

LISTING A.2: loop1.py

```
import numpy as np

list = [1,2,3]
arr1 = np.array([1,2,3])

for e in list:
  print(e)

for e in arr1:
  print(e)
```

Listing A.2 initializes the variable `list`, which is a list, and also the variable `arr1`, which is an array. The next portion of Listing A.2 contains two loops, each of which iterates through the elements in `list` and `arr1`. The syntax is identical in both loops. The output from launching Listing A.2 is here:

```
1
2
3
1
2
3
```

APPENDING ELEMENTS TO ARRAYS (1)

Listing A.3 shows the content of `append1.py` that illustrates how to append elements to a NumPy array.

LISTING A.3: append1.py

```
import numpy as np

arr1 = np.array([1,2,3])

# these do not work:
#arr1.append(4)
#arr1 = arr1 + [5]

arr1 = np.append(arr1,4)
arr1 = np.append(arr1,[5])

for e in arr1:
  print(e)
```

```
arr2 = arr1 + arr1

for e in arr2:
   print(e)
```

Listing A.3 initializes the variable `list`, which is a Python list, and also the variable `arr1`, which is a NumPy array. The output from launching Listing A.3 is as follows:

```
1
2
3
4
5
2
4
6
8
10
```

APPENDING ELEMENTS TO ARRAYS (2)

Listing A.4 shows the content of `append2.py`, which illustrates how to append elements to a NumPy array and a Python list.

LISTING A.4: append2.py

```
import numpy as np

arr1 = np.array([1,2,3])
arr1 = np.append(arr1,4)

for e in arr1:
   print(e)

arr1 = np.array([1,2,3])
arr1 = np.append(arr1,4)

arr2 = arr1 + arr1

for e in arr2:
   print(e)
```

Listing A.4 initializes the variable `arr1`, which is a NumPy array. Notice that NumPy arrays do not have an "append" method: this method is available through NumPy itself. Another important difference between Python lists and NumPy arrays is that the "+" operator concatenates Python lists, whereas this operator doubles the elements in a NumPy array. The output from launching Listing A.4 is as follows:

```
1
2
3
4
```

```
2
4
6
8
```

MULTIPLYING LISTS AND ARRAYS

Listing A.5 shows the content of `multiply1.py` that illustrates how to multiply elements in a Python list and a NumPy array.

LISTING A.5: multiply1.py

```
import numpy as np

list1 = [1,2,3]
arr1  = np.array([1,2,3])
print('list:  ',list1)
print('arr1:  ',arr1)
print('2*list:',2*list)
print('2*arr1:',2*arr1)
```

Listing A.5 contains a Python list called `list` and a NumPy array called `arr1`. The `print()` statements display the contents of `list` and `arr1`, as well as the result of doubling `list1` and `arr1`. Recall that "doubling" a Python list is different from doubling a Python array, which you can see in the output from launching Listing A.5:

```
('list:  ', [1, 2, 3])
('arr1:  ', array([1, 2, 3]))
('2*list:', [1, 2, 3, 1, 2, 3])
('2*arr1:', array([2, 4, 6]))
```

DOUBLING THE ELEMENTS IN A LIST

Listing A.6 shows the content of `double_list1.py`, which illustrates how to double the elements in a Python list.

LISTING A.6: double_list1.py

```
import numpy as np

list1 = [1,2,3]
list2 = []

for e in list1:
  list2.append(2*e)

print('list1:',list1)
print('list2:',list2)
```

Listing A.6 contains a Python list called `list1` and an empty NumPy list called `list2`. The next code snippet iterates through the elements of `list1` and appends them to the variable list2. The pair of `print()` statements display the contents of `list1` and `list2` to show you that they are the same. The output from launching Listing A.6 is here:

```
('list: ', [1, 2, 3])
('list2:', [2, 4, 6])
```

LISTS AND EXPONENTS

Listing A.7 shows the content of `exponent_list1.py`, which illustrates how to compute exponents of the elements in a Python list.

LISTING A.7: exponent_list1.py

```
import numpy as np

list1 = [1,2,3]
list2 = []

for e in list1:
  list2.append(e*e) # e*e = squared

print('list1:',list1)
print('list2:',list2)
```

Listing A.7 contains a Python list called `list1` and an empty list called `list2`. The next code snippet iterates through the elements of `list1` and appends the square of each element to the variable `list2`. The pair of `print()` statements display the contents of `list1` and `list2`. The output from launching Listing A.7 is here:

```
('list1:', [1, 2, 3])
('list2:', [1, 4, 9])
```

ARRAYS AND EXPONENTS

Listing A.8 shows the content of `exponent_array1.py`, which illustrates how to compute exponents of the elements in a NumPy array.

LISTING A.8: exponent_array1.py

```
import numpy as np

arr1 = np.array([1,2,3])
arr2 = arr1**2
arr3 = arr1**3

print('arr1:',arr1)
print('arr2:',arr2)
print('arr3:',arr3)
```

Listing A.8 contains a NumPy array called `arr1`, followed by two NumPy arrays called `arr2` and `arr3`. Notice the compact manner in which `arr2` is initialized with the square of the elements in `arr1`, followed by the initialization of `arr3` with the cube of the elements in `arr1`. The three `print()` statements display the contents of `arr1`, `arr2`, and `arr3`. The output from launching Listing A.8 is here:

```
('arr1:', array([1, 2, 3]))
('arr2:', array([1, 4, 9]))
('arr3:', array([ 1,  8, 27]))
```

MATH OPERATIONS AND ARRAYS

Listing A.9 shows the content of `mathops_array1.py` that illustrate how to compute exponents of the elements in a NumPy array.

LISTING A.9: mathops_array1.py

```
import numpy as np

arr1 = np.array([1,2,3])
sqrt = np.sqrt(arr1)
log1 = np.log(arr1)
exp1 = np.exp(arr1)

print('sqrt:',sqrt)
print('log1:',log1)
print('exp1:',exp1)
```

Listing A.9 contains a NumPy array called `arr1`, followed by three arrays called `sqrt`, `log1`, and `exp1` that are initialized with the square root, the log, and the exponential value of the elements in `arr1`, respectively. The three `print()` statements display the contents of `sqrt`, `log1`, and `exp1`. The output from launching Listing A.9 is here:

```
('sqrt:', array([1.        , 1.41421356, 1.73205081]))
('log1:', array([0.        , 0.69314718, 1.09861229]))
('exp1:', array([2.71828183, 7.3890561 , 20.08553692]))
```

WORKING WITH "−1" SUB-RANGES WITH VECTORS

Listing A.10 shows the content of `npsubarray2.py`, which illustrates how to compute exponents of the elements in a NumPy array.

LISTING A.10: npsubarray2.py

```
import numpy as np

# -1 => "all except the last element in ..." (row or col)

arr1  = np.array([1,2,3,4,5])
print('arr1:',arr1)
print('arr1[0:-1]:',arr1[0:-1])
print('arr1[1:-1]:',arr1[1:-1])
print('arr1[::-1]:', arr1[::-1]) # reverse!
```

Listing A.10 contains a NumPy array called `arr1`, followed by four `print()` statements, each of which displays a different sub-range of values in `arr1`. The output from launching Listing A.10 is as follows:

```
('arr1:',        array([1, 2, 3, 4, 5]))
('arr1[0:-1]:', array([1, 2, 3, 4]))
('arr1[1:-1]:', array([2, 3, 4]))
('arr1[::-1]:', array([5, 4, 3, 2, 1]))
```

WORKING WITH "–1" SUB-RANGES WITH ARRAYS

Listing A.11 shows the content of `np2darray2.py`, which illustrates how to compute exponents of the elements in a NumPy array.

LISTING A.11: np2darray2.py

```
import numpy as np

# -1 => "the last element in ..." (row or col)

arr1  = np.array([(1,2,3),(4,5,6),(7,8,9),(10,11,12)])
print('arr1:',        arr1)
print('arr1[-1,:]:',  arr1[-1,:])
print('arr1[:,-1]:',  arr1[:,-1])
print('arr1[-1:,-1]:',arr1[-1:,-1])
```

Listing A.11 contains a NumPy array called `arr1`, followed by four `print` statements, each of which displays a different sub-range of values in `arr1`. The output from launching Listing A.11 is shown here:

```
(arr1:', array([[1,   2,   3],
                [4,   5,   6],
                [7,   8,   9],
                [10, 11, 12]]))
(arr1[-1,:]]',   array([10, 11, 12]))
(arr1[:,-1]:',   array([3,   6,   9, 12]))
(arr1[-1:,-1]]', array([12]))
```

OTHER USEFUL NUMPY METHODS

The following methods are very useful.

- The method `np.zeros()` initializes an array with 0 values.
- The method `np.ones()` initializes an array with 1 value.
- The method `np.empty()` initializes an array with 0 values.
- The method `np.arange()` provides a range of numbers.
- The method `np.shape()` displays the shape of an object.
- The method `np.reshape()` (*Very useful!*)
- The method `np.linspace()` (*Useful in regression!*)

- The method np.mean() computes the mean of a set of numbers.
- The method np.std() computes the standard deviation of a set of numbers.

Although the np.zeros() and np.empty() both initialize a 2D array with 0, np.zeros() requires less execution time. You could also use np.full(size, 0), but this method is the slowest of all three methods.

The reshape() method and the linspace() method are useful for changing the dimensions of an array and generating a list of numeric values, respectively. The reshape() method often appears in TensorFlow code, and the linspace() method is useful for generating a set of numbers in linear regression.

The mean() and std() methods are useful for calculating the mean and the standard deviation of a set of numbers. For example, you can use these two methods to resize the values in a Gaussian distribution so that their mean is 0 and the standard deviation is 1. This process is called *standardizing* a Gaussian distribution.

ARRAYS AND VECTOR OPERATIONS

Listing A.12 shows the content of array_vector.py that illustrates how to perform vector operations on the elements in a NumPy array.

LISTING A.12: array_vector.py

```
import numpy as np

a = np.array([[1,2], [3, 4]])
b = np.array([[5,6], [7,8]])

print('a:         ', a)
print('b:         ', b)
print('a + b:     ', a+b)
print('a - b:     ', a-b)
print('a * b:     ', a*b)
print('a / b:     ', a/b)
print('b / a:     ', b/a)
print('a.dot(b):',a.dot(b))
```

Listing A.12 contains two NumPy arrays called a and b, followed by eight print() statements, each of which displays the result of applying a different arithmetic operation to the arrays a and b. The output from launching Listing A.12 is here:

```
('a     :  ', array([[1, 2], [3, 4]]))
('b     :  ', array([[5, 6], [7, 8]]))
('a + b:  ', array([[ 6,  8], [10, 12]]))
('a - b:  ', array([[-4, -4], [-4, -4]]))
('a * b:  ', array([[ 5, 12], [21, 32]]))
('a / b:  ', array([[0, 0], [0, 0]]))
('b / a:  ', array([[5, 3], [2, 2]]))
('a.dot(b):', array([[19, 22], [43, 50]]))
```

NUMPY AND DOT PRODUCTS (1)

Listing A.13 shows the content of `dotproduct1.py`, which illustrates how to perform the dot product on the elements in a NumPy array.

LISTING A.13: dotproduct1.py

```
import numpy as np

a = np.array([1,2])
b = np.array([2,3])

dot2 = 0
for e,f in zip(a,b):
  dot2 += e*f

print('a:    ',a)
print('b:    ',b)
print('a*b: ',a*b)
print('dot1:',a.dot(b))
print('dot2:',dot2)
```

Listing A.13 contains two NumPy arrays called a and b, followed by a simple loop that computes the dot product of a and b. The next section contains five `print()` statements that display the contents of a and b, as well as their inner product that is calculated in three different ways. The output from launching Listing A.13 is as follows:

```
('a:    ', array([1, 2]))
('b:    ', array([2, 3]))
('a*b: ', array([2, 6]))
('dot1:', 8)
('dot2:', 8)
```

NUMPY AND DOT PRODUCTS (2)

NumPy arrays support a "dot" method for calculating the inner product of an array of numbers, which uses the same formula that you use for calculating the inner product of a pair of vectors. Listing A.14 shows the content of `dotproduct2.py` that illustrates how to calculate the dot product of two NumPy arrays.

LISTING A.14: dotproduct2.py

```
import numpy as np

a = np.array([1,2])
b = np.array([2,3])

print('a:          ',a)
print('b:          ',b)
print('a.dot(b):   ',a.dot(b))
```

```
print('b.dot(a):    ',b.dot(a))
print('np.dot(a,b):',np.dot(a,b))
print('np.dot(b,a):',np.dot(b,a))
```

Listing A.14 contains two NumPy arrays called a and b, followed by six `print()` statements that display the contents of a and b, as well as their inner product that is calculated in three different ways. The output from launching Listing A.14 is as follows:

```
('a:             ', array([1, 2]))
('b:             ', array([2, 3]))
('a.dot(b):      ', 8)
('b.dot(a):      ', 8)
('np.dot(a,b):', 8)
('np.dot(b,a):', 8)
```

NUMPY AND THE LENGTH OF VECTORS

The *norm* of a vector (or an array of numbers) is the length of a vector, which is the square root of the dot product of a vector with itself. NumPy also provides the sum and square functions that you can use to calculate the norm of a vector.

Listing A.15 shows the content of `array_norm.py`, which illustrates how to calculate the magnitude ("norm") of a NumPy array of numbers.

LISTING A.15: array_norm.py

```
import numpy as np

a = np.array([2,3])
asquare = np.square(a)
asqsum  = np.sum(np.square(a))
anorm1  = np.sqrt(np.sum(a*a))
anorm2  = np.sqrt(np.sum(np.square(a)))
anorm3  = np.linalg.norm(a)

print('a:       ',a)
print('asquare:',asquare)
print('asqsum: ',asqsum)
print('anorm1: ',anorm1)
print('anorm2: ',anorm2)
print('anorm3: ',anorm3)
```

Listing A.15 contains an initial NumPy array called a, followed by the array asquare and the numeric values asqsum, anorm1, anorm2, and anorm3. The array asquare contains the square of the elements in the array a, and the numeric value asqsum contains the sum of the elements in the array asquare. Next, the numeric value anorm1 equals the square root of the sum of the square of the elements in a. The numeric value anorm2 is the same as anorm1, computed in a slightly different fashion. Finally, the numeric value anorm3 is equal to anorm2, but as you can see, anorm3 is calculated via a single method, whereas anorm2 requires a succession of methods.

The last portion of Listing A.15 consists of six `print()` statements, each of which displays the computed values. The output from launching Listing A.15 is shown here:

```
('a:         ', array([2, 3]))
('asquare:', array([4, 9]))
('asqsum: ', 13)
('anorm1: ', 3.605551275463989)
('anorm2: ', 3.605551275463989)
('anorm3: ', 3.605551275463989)
```

NUMPY AND OTHER OPERATIONS

NumPy provides the * operator to multiply the components of two vectors to produce a third vector whose components are the products of the corresponding components of the initial pair of vectors. This operation is called a *Hadamard product*, named after a famous mathematician. If you then add the components of the third vector, the sum is equal to the inner product of the initial pair of vectors.

Listing A.16 shows the content of `otherops.py`, which illustrates how to perform other operations on a NumPy array.

LISTING A.16: otherops.py

```
import numpy as np

a = np.array([1,2])
b = np.array([3,4])

print('a:           ',a)
print('b:           ',b)
print('a*b:         ',a*b)
print('np.sum(a*b): ',np.sum(a*b))
print('(a*b.sum()): ',(a*b).sum())
```

Listing A.16 contains two NumPy arrays called a and b, followed by five `print()` statements that display the contents of a and b, as well as their Hadamard product and their inner product that is calculated in two different ways. The output from launching Listing A.16 is as follows:

```
('a:           ', array([1, 2]))
('b:           ', array([3, 4]))
('a*b:         ', array([3, 8]))
('np.sum(a*b): ', 11)
('(a*b.sum()): ', 11)
```

NUMPY AND THE RESHAPE() METHOD

NumPy arrays support the `reshape()` method that allows you to restructure the dimensions of an array of numbers. In general, if an array contains m elements, where m is a positive integer, then that array can be restructured as an m1 x m2 array, where m1 and m2 are positive integers such that m1*m2 = m.

Listing A.17 shows the content of `numpy_reshape.py` that illustrates how to use the `reshape()` method on a NumPy array.

LISTING A.17: numpy_reshape.py

```
import numpy as np

x = np.array([[2, 3], [4, 5], [6, 7]])
print(x.shape) # (3, 2)

x = x.reshape((2, 3))
print(x.shape) # (2, 3)
print('x1:',x)

x = x.reshape((-1))
print(x.shape) # (6,)
print('x2:',x)

x = x.reshape((6, -1))
print(x.shape) # (6, 1)
print('x3:',x)

x = x.reshape((-1, 6))
print(x.shape) # (1, 6)
print('x4:',x)
```

Listing A.17 contains a NumPy array called x whose dimensions are 3x2, followed by a set of invocations of the `reshape()` method that reshape the contents of x. The first invocation of the `reshape()` method changes the shape of x from 3x2 to 2x3. The second invocation changes the shape of x from 2x3 to 6x1. The third invocation changes the shape of x from 1x6 to 6x1. The final invocation changes the shape of x from 6x1 to 1x6 again.

Each invocation of the `reshape()` method is followed by a `print()` statement so that you can see the effect of the invocation. The output from launching Listing A.17 is as follows:

```
(3, 2)
(2, 3)
('x1:', array([[2, 3, 4],
       [5, 6, 7]]))
(6,)
('x2:', array([2, 3, 4, 5, 6, 7]))
(6, 1)
('x3:', array([[2],
       [3],
       [4],
       [5],
       [6],
       [7]]))
(1, 6)
```

CALCULATING THE MEAN AND STANDARD DEVIATION

If you need to review these concepts from statistics (and perhaps also the mean, median, and mode, as well), please read the appropriate on-line tutorials.

NumPy provides various built-in functions that perform statistical calculations, such as the following:

- `np.linspace()` <= useful for regression
- `np.mean()`
- `np.std()`

The `np.linspace()` method generates a set of equally spaced numbers between a lower bound and an upper bound. The `np.mean()` and `np.std()` methods calculate the mean and standard deviation, respectively, of a set of numbers. Listing A.18 shows the content of `sample_mean_std.py`, which illustrates how to calculate statistical values from a NumPy array.

LISTING A.18: sample_mean_std.py

```
import numpy as np

x2 = np.arange(8)
print('mean = ',x2.mean())
print('std  = ',x2.std())

x3 = (x2 - x2.mean())/x2.std()
print('x3 mean = ',x3.mean())
print('x3 std  = ',x3.std())
```

Listing A.18 contains a NumPy array `x2` that consists of the first eight integers. Next, the `mean()` and `std()` that are associated with `x2` are invoked to calculate the mean and standard deviation, respectively, of the elements of `x2`. The output from launching Listing A.18 is here:

```
('a:           ', array([1, 2]))
('b:           ', array([3, 4]))
```

CODE SAMPLE WITH MEAN AND STANDARD DEVIATION

The code sample in this section extends the code sample in the previous section with additional statistical values, and the code in Listing A.19 can be used for any data distribution. The code sample uses random numbers simply for the purposes of illustration. After you have launched the code sample, replace those numbers with values from a CSV file or some other dataset containing meaningful values.

This section does not provide details regarding the meaning of quartiles, but you can learn about quartiles online:

https://en.wikipedia.org/wiki/Quartile

Listing A.19 shows the content of `stat_values.py` that illustrates how to display various statistical values from a NumPy array of random numbers.

LISTING A.19: stat_values.py

```
import numpy as np

from numpy import percentile
from numpy.random import rand

# generate data sample
data = np.random.rand(1000)

# calculate quartiles, min, and max
quartiles = percentile(data, [25, 50, 75])
data_min, data_max = data.min(), data.max()

# print summary information
print('Minimum:   %.3f' % data_min)
print('Q1 value: %.3f' % quartiles[0])
print('Median:    %.3f' % quartiles[1])
print('Mean Val: %.3f' % data.mean())
print('Std Dev:   %.3f' % data.std())
print('Q3 value: %.3f' % quartiles[2])
print('Maximum:   %.3f' % data_max)
```

The data sample (shown in bold) in Listing A.19 is from a uniform distribution between 0 and 1. The `percentile()` function calculates a linear interpolation (average) between observations, which is needed to calculate the median of a sample with an even number of values. The functions `min()` and `max()` calculate the smallest and largest values in the data sample. The output from launching Listing A.19 is here:

```
Minimum:   0.000
Q1 value: 0.237
Median:    0.500
Mean Val: 0.495
Std Dev:   0.295
Q3 value: 0.747
Maximum:   0.999
```

Trimmed Mean and Weighted Mean

In addition to the arithmetic mean, there are variants that are known as the weighted mean and a trimmed mean (also called a truncated mean).

A *trimmed mean* is a robust estimate (i.e., a metric that is not sensitive to outliers). As a simple example of a trimmed mean, suppose that you have five scores for the evaluation of a product. Exclude the highest and lowest scores and then compute the average of the remaining three scores. If you have multiple sets of five scores, repeat the preceding process and then compute the average of the set of trimmed mean values.

A *weighted mean* is useful when sample data does not represent different groups in a dataset. Assigning a larger weight to groups that are under-represented yields a weighted mean that more accurately represents the various groups in the dataset. However, keep in mind that outliers can affect the mean as well as the weighted mean.

The weighted mean is the same as the expected value. If you are unfamiliar with the notion of an expected value, suppose that the set P = {p1,p2,...,pn} is a probability distribution, which means that the numeric values in the set P must be non-negative and have a sum equal to 1. In addition, suppose that V = {v1,v2,...,vn} is a set of numeric scores that are assigned to n features of a product M. The values in the set V are probably positive integers in some range (e.g., between 1 and 10).

Then the *expected value* E for that product is computed as follows:

```
E = p1*v1 + p2*v2 + ... + pn*vn
```

SUMMARY

This appendix introduced you to the NumPy library for Python. You learned how to write Python scripts containing loops, arrays, and lists. You also saw how to work with dot products and the reshape() method.

Then you learned how to work with sub-ranges of arrays, as well as negative sub-ranges of vectors and arrays, both of which are useful for extracting portions of datasets in machine learning tasks. You also saw other NumPy operations, such as the reshape() method, which is extremely useful (and very common) when working with images files.

APPENDIX B

INTRODUCTION TO PANDAS

This appendix introduces you to Pandas and provides code samples that illustrate some of its useful features. If you are familiar with these topics, skim through the material and peruse the code samples, just in case they contain information that is new to you.

The first part of this appendix contains a brief introduction to Pandas. This section contains code samples that illustrate some features of data frames and a brief discussion of series, which are two of the main features of Pandas.

The second part of this appendix discusses various types of data frames that you can create, such as numeric and Boolean data frames. In addition, we discuss examples of creating data frames with NumPy functions and random numbers.

NOTE *Several code samples in this appendix reference the NumPy library for working with arrays and generating random numbers, which is discussed in Appendix A.*

WHAT IS PANDAS?

Pandas is a Python package that is compatible with other Python packages, such as NumPy and Matplotlib. Install Pandas by opening a command shell and invoking this command for Python 3.x:

```
pip3 install pandas
```

In many ways, the semantics of the APIs in the Pandas library are similar to a spreadsheet, along with support for XSL, XML, HTML, and CSV file types. Pandas provides a data type called a data frame (similar to a Python dictionary), which has an extremely powerful functionality.

Pandas data frames support a variety of input types, such as ndarray, list, dict, or series.

The data type series is another mechanism for managing data. In addition to performing an online search for more details regarding Series, the following article contains a good introduction:

https://towardsdatascience.com/20-examples-to-master-pandas-series-bc4c68200324

Options and Settings

You can change the default values of environment variables, an example of which is shown here:

```
import pandas as pd

display_settings = {
    'max_columns': 8,
    'expand_frame_repr': True,  # Wrap to multiple pages
    'max_rows': 20,
    'precision': 3,
    'show_dimensions': True
}

for op, value in display_settings.items():
    pd.set_option("display.{}".format(op), value)
```

Include the preceding code block in your own code if you want Pandas to display a maximum of 20 rows and 8 columns, and floating point numbers displayed with 3 decimal places. Set expand_frame_rep to True if you want the output to "wrap around" to multiple pages. The preceding for loop iterates through display_settings and sets the options equal to their corresponding values.

In addition, the following code snippet displays all Pandas options and their current values in your code:

```
print(pd.describe_option())
```

There are various other operations that you can perform with options and their values (such as the pd.reset() method for resetting values), as described in the Pandas user guide:

https://pandas.pydata.org/pandas-docs/stable/user_guide/options.html

Data Frames

In simplified terms, a Pandas data frame is a two-dimensional data structure, and it is convenient to think of the data structure in terms of rows and columns. Data frames can be labeled (rows as well as columns), and the columns can contain different data types. The source of the dataset for a Pandas data frame can be a data file, a database table, and a Web service. The data frame features include:

- Data frame methods
- Data frame statistics
- Grouping, pivoting, and reshaping
- Handling missing data
- Joining data frames

The code samples in this appendix show you almost all the features in the preceding list.

Data Frames and Data Cleaning Tasks

The specific tasks that you need to perform depend on the structure and contents of a dataset. In general, you perform a workflow with the following steps, not necessarily always in this order (and some might be optional). All of the following steps can be performed with a Pandas data frame:

- Read data into a data frame
- Display the top of the data frame
- Display column data types
- Display missing values
- Replace "NA" with a value
- Iterate through the columns
- Show statistics for each column
- Find missing values
- Find the total missing values
- Find the percentage of missing values
- Sort the table values
- Print summary information
- Show columns with > 50% of the data missing
- Rename columns

This appendix contains sections that illustrate how to perform many of the steps in the preceding list.

Alternatives to Pandas

Before delving into the code samples, there are alternatives to Pandas that offer very useful features, some of which are shown here:

- `PySpark` (for large datasets)
- `Dask` (for distributed processing)
- `Modin` (faster performance)
- `Datatable` (R `data.table` for Python)

The inclusion of these alternatives is not intended to diminish Pandas. Indeed, you might not need any of the functionality in the preceding list. However, you might need such functionality in the future, so you should know about these alternatives now (and there may be even more powerful alternatives at some point in the future).

A DATA FRAME WITH A NUMPY EXAMPLE

Listing B.1 shows the content of `pandas_df.py` that illustrates how to define several data frames and display their contents.

LISTING B.1: pandas_df.py

```python
import pandas as pd
import numpy as np

myvector1 = np.array([1,2,3,4,5])
print("myvector1:")
print(myvector1)
print()

mydf1 = pd.DataFrame(myvector1)
print("mydf1:")
print(mydf1)
print()

myvector2 = np.array([i for i in range(1,6)])
print("myvector2:")
print(myvector2)
print()

mydf2 = pd.DataFrame(myvector2)
print("mydf2:")
print(mydf2)
print()

myarray = np.array([[10,30,20], [50,40,60],[1000,2000,3000]])
print("myarray:")
print(myarray)
print()

mydf3 = pd.DataFrame(myarray)
print("mydf3:")
print(mydf3)
print()
```

Listing B.1 starts with standard `import` statements for Pandas and NumPy, followed by the definition of two one-dimensional NumPy arrays and a two-dimensional NumPy array. Each NumPy variable is followed by a corresponding Pandas data frame (`mydf1`, `mydf2`, and `mydf3`). Launch the code in Listing B.1 to see the following output, and you can compare the NumPy arrays with the Pandas data frames:

```
myvector1:
[1 2 3 4 5]

mydf1:
   0
0  1
1  2
2  3
3  4
4  5

myvector2:
[1 2 3 4 5]
```

```
mydf2:
   0
0  1
1  2
2  3
3  4
4  5


myarray:
[[  10   30   20]
 [  50   40   60]
 [1000 2000 3000]]


mydf3:
        0     1     2
0      10    30    20
1      50    40    60
2    1000  2000  3000
```

By contrast, the following code block illustrates how to define two Pandas `Series` that are part of the definition of a data frame:

```
names = pd.Series(['SF', 'San Jose', 'Sacramento'])
sizes = pd.Series([852469, 1015785, 485199])
df = pd.Data frame({ 'Cities': names, 'Size': sizes })
print(df)
```

Create a Python file with the preceding code (along with the required `import` statement), and when you launch that code, you will see the following output:

```
     City name      sizes
0           SF     852469
1     San Jose    1015785
2    Sacramento    485199
```

DESCRIBING A DATA FRAME

Listing B.2 shows the content of `pandas_df_describe.py`, which illustrates how to define a Pandas data frame that contains a 3x3 NumPy array of integer values, where the rows and columns of the data frame are labeled. Other aspects of the data frame are also displayed.

LISTING B.2: pandas_df_describe.py

```
import numpy as np
import pandas as pd

myarray = np.array([[10,30,20], [50,40,60],[1000,2000,3000]])

rownames = ['apples', 'oranges', 'beer']
colnames = ['January', 'February', 'March']
```

```
mydf = pd.DataFrame(myarray, index=rownames, columns=colnames)
print("contents of df:")
print(mydf)
print()

print("contents of January:")
print(mydf['January'])
print()

print("Number of Rows:")
print(mydf.shape[0])
print()

print("Number of Columns:")
print(mydf.shape[1])
print()

print("Number of Rows and Columns:")
print(mydf.shape)
print()

print("Column Names:")
print(mydf.columns)
print()

print("Column types:")
print(mydf.dtypes)
print()

print("Description:")
print(mydf.describe())
print()
```

Listing B.2 starts with two standard `import` statements followed by the variable `myarray`, which is a 3x3 NumPy array of numbers. The variables `rownames` and `colnames` provide names for the rows and columns, respectively, of the Pandas data frame `mydf`, which is initialized as a Pandas data frame with the specified data source (i.e., `myarray`).

The first portion of the output below requires a single `print()` statement (which simply displays the contents of `mydf`). The second portion of the output is generated by invoking the `describe()` method that is available for any Pandas data frame. The `describe()` method is useful: you will see various statistical quantities, such as the mean, standard deviation minimum, and maximum performed by *columns* (not rows), along with values for the 25th, 50th, and 75th percentiles. The output of Listing B.2 is here:

```
contents of df:
        January  February  March
apples       10        30     20
oranges      50        40     60
beer       1000      2000   3000

contents of January:
apples       10
oranges      50
```

```
beer          1000
Name: January, dtype: int64

Number of Rows:
3

Number of Columns:
3

Number of Rows and Columns:
(3, 3)

Column Names:
Index(['January', 'February', 'March'], dtype='object')

Column types:
January      int64
February     int64
March        int64
dtype: object

Description:
          January     February        March
count    3.000000     3.000000     3.000000
mean   353.333333   690.000000  1026.666667
std    560.386771  1134.504297  1709.073823
min     10.000000    30.000000    20.000000
25%     30.000000    35.000000    40.000000
50%     50.000000    40.000000    60.000000
75%    525.000000  1020.000000  1530.000000
max   1000.000000  2000.000000  3000.000000
```

BOOLEAN DATA FRAMES

Pandas supports Boolean operations on data frames, such as the logical OR, the logical AND, and the logical negation of a pair of data frames. Listing B.3 shows the content of pandas_boolean_df.py that illustrates how to define a data frame whose rows and columns are Boolean values.

LISTING B.3: pandas_boolean_df.py

```
import pandas as pd

df1 = pd.DataFrame({'a': [1, 0, 1], 'b': [0, 1, 1] }, dtype=bool)
df2 = pd.DataFrame({'a': [0, 1, 1], 'b': [1, 1, 0] }, dtype=bool)

print("df1 & df2:")
print(df1 & df2)

print("df1 | df2:")
print(df1 | df2)

print("df1 ^ df2:")
print(df1 ^ df2)
```

Listing B.3 initializes the data frames `df1` and `df2`, and then computes `df1 & df2`, `df1 | df2`, and `df1 ^ df2`, which represent the logical AND, the logical OR, and the logical negation, respectively, of `df1` and `df2`. The output from launching the code in Listing B.3 is as follows:

```
df1 & df2:
        a       b
0   False   False
1   False    True
2    True   False
df1 | df2:
        a       b
0    True    True
1    True    True
2    True    True
df1 ^ df2:
        a       b
0    True    True
1    True   False
2   False    True
```

Transposing a Data Frame

The T attribute (as well as the transpose function) enables you to generate the transpose of a data frame, similar to the NumPy ndarray. The transpose operation switches rows to columns and columns to rows. For example, the following code snippet defines a Pandas data frame `df1` and then displays the transpose of `df1`:

```
df1 = pd.DataFrame({'a': [1, 0, 1], 'b': [0, 1, 1] }, dtype=int)

print("df1.T:")
print(df1.T)
```

The output of the preceding code snippet is here:

```
df1.T:
     0   1   2
a    1   0   1
b    0   1   1
```

The following code snippet defines the data frames `df1 and df2` and then displays their sum:

```
df1 = pd.DataFrame({'a' : [1, 0, 1], 'b' : [0, 1, 1] }, dtype=int)
df2 = pd.DataFrame({'a' : [3, 3, 3], 'b' : [5, 5, 5] }, dtype=int)

print("df1 + df2:")
print(df1 + df2)
```

The output is here:

```
df1 + df2:
     a   b
0    4   5
1    3   6
2    4   6
```

DATA FRAMES AND RANDOM NUMBERS

Listing B.4 shows the content of `pandas_random_df.py` that illustrates how to create a Pandas data frame with random integers.

LISTING B.4: pandas_random_df.py

```
import pandas as pd
import numpy as np

df = pd.DataFrame(np.random.randint(1, 5, size=(5, 2)),
columns=['a','b'])
df = df.append(df.agg(['sum', 'mean']))

print("Contents of data frame:")
print(df)
```

Listing B.4 defines the data frame `df`, which consists of 5 rows and 2 columns of random integers between 1 and 5. Notice that the columns of `df` are labeled "a" and "b." In addition, the next code snippet appends two rows consisting of the sum and the mean of the numbers in both columns. The output of Listing B.4 is here:

```
a      b
0       1.0   2.0
1       1.0   1.0
2       4.0   3.0
3       3.0   1.0
4       1.0   2.0
sum    10.0   9.0
mean    2.0   1.8
```

Listing B.5 shows the content of `pandas_combine_df.py` that illustrates how to combine the data frames.

LISTING B.5: pandas_combine_df.py

```
import pandas as pd
import numpy as np

df = pd.DataFrame({'foo1' : np.random.randn(5),
                   'foo2' : np.random.randn(5)})

print("contents of df:")
print(df)

print("contents of foo1:")
print(df.foo1)

print("contents of foo2:")
print(df.foo2)
```

Listing B.5 defines the data frame df that consists of 5 rows and 2 columns (labeled "foo1" and "foo2") of random real numbers between 0 and 5. The next portion of Listing B.5 shows the content of df and foo1. The output of Listing B.5 is as follows:

```
contents of df:
        foo1        foo2
0   0.274680  _0.848669
1  _0.399771  _0.814679
2   0.454443  _0.363392
3   0.473753   0.550849
4  _0.211783  _0.015014
contents of foo1:
0      0.256773
1      1.204322
2      1.040515
3     _0.518414
4      0.634141
Name: foo1, dtype: float64
contents of foo2:
0     _2.506550
1     _0.896516
2     _0.222923
3      0.934574
4      0.527033
Name: foo2, dtype: float64
```

READING CSV FILES

Pandas provides the read_csv() method for reading the contents of CSV files. For example, Listing B.6 shows the content of sometext.csv that contains labeled data (spam or ham). Listing B.7 shows the content of read_csv_file.py that illustrates how to read the contents of a CSV file.

LISTING B.6: sometext.csv

```
type    text
ham     Available only for today
ham     I'm joking with you
spam    Free entry in 2 a wkly comp
ham     U dun say so early hor
ham     I don't think he goes to usf
spam    FreeMsg Hey there
ham     my brother is not sick
ham     As per your request Melle
spam    WINNER!! As a valued customer
```

LISTING B.7: read_csv_file.py

```
import pandas as pd
import numpy as np

df = pd.read_csv('sometext.csv', delimiter='\t')

print("=> First five rows:")
print(df.head(5))
```

Listing B.7 reads the contents of `sometext.csv`, whose columns are separated by a tab ("\t") delimiter. Launch the code in Listing B.7 to see the following output:

```
=> First five rows:
   type                          text
0  ham       Available only for today
1  ham              I'm joking with you
2  spam    Free entry in 2 a wkly comp
3  ham             U dun say so early hor
4  ham    I don't think he goes to usf
```

The default value for the `head()` method is 5, but you can display the first n rows of a data frame `df` with the code snippet `df.head(n)`.

Specifying a Separator and Column Sets in Text Files

The previous section showed you how to use the `delimiter` attribute to specify the delimiter in a text file. You can also use the `sep` parameter specifies a different separator. In addition, you can assign the `names` parameter the column names in the data that you want to read. An example of using `delimiter` and `sep` is here:

```
df2 = pd.read_csv("data.csv",sep="|",
           names=["Name","Surname","Height","Weight"])
```

Pandas also provides the `read_table()` method for reading the contents of CSV files, which uses the same syntax as the `read_csv()` method.

Specifying an Index in Text Files

Suppose that you know that a particular column in a text file contains the index value for the rows in the text file. For example, a text file that contains the data in a relational table would typically contain an index column.

Fortunately, Pandas allows you to specify the kth column as the index in a text file, as shown here:

```
df = pd.read_csv('myfile.csv', index_col=k)
```

THE loc() AND iloc() METHODS

If you want to display the contents of a record in a Pandas data frame, specify the index of the row in the `loc()` method. For example, the following code snippet displays the data by feature name in a data frame `df`:

```
df.loc[feature_name]
```

Select the first row of the "height" column in the data frame:

```
df.loc([0], ['height'])
```

The following code snippet uses the `iloc()` function to display the first 8 records of the name column with this code snippet:

```
df.iloc[0:8]['name']
```

CONVERTING CATEGORICAL DATA TO NUMERIC DATA

One common task (especially in machine learning) involves converting a feature containing character data into a feature that contains numeric data. Listing B.8 shows the content of cat-2numeric.py that illustrates how to replace a text field with a corresponding numeric field.

LISTING B.8: cat2numeric.py

```
import pandas as pd
import numpy as np

df = pd.read_csv('sometext.csv', delimiter='\t')

print("=> First five rows (before):")
print(df.head(5))
print("------------------------")
print()

# map ham/spam to 0/1 values:
df['type'] = df['type'].map( {'ham':0 , 'spam':1} )

print("=> First five rows (after):")
print(df.head(5))
print("------------------------")
```

Listing B.8 initializes the data frame df with the contents of the CSV file sometext.csv, and then displays the contents of the first five rows by invoking df.head(5), which is also the default number of rows to display.

The next code snippet in Listing B.8 invokes the map() method to replace occurrences of ham with 0 and replace occurrences of spam with 1 in the column labeled type, as shown here:

```
df['type'] = df['type'].map( {'ham':0 , 'spam':1} )
```

The last portion of Listing B.8 invokes the head() method again to display the first five rows of the dataset after having renamed the contents of the column type. Launch the code in Listing B.8 to see the following output:

```
=> First five rows (before):
   type                       text
0  ham      Available only for today
1  ham             I'm joking with you
2  spam   Free entry in 2 a wkly comp
3  ham          U dun say so early hor
4  ham   I don't think he goes to usf
------------------------

=> First five rows (after):
   type                       text
0   0       Available only for today
1   0              I'm joking with you
2   1    Free entry in 2 a wkly comp
```

```
3      0         U dun say so early hor
4      0  I don't think he goes to usf
```

As another example, Listing B.9 shows the contents of shirts.csv and Listing B.10 shows the contents of shirts.py. These examples illustrate four techniques for converting categorical data into numeric data.

LISTING B.9: shirts.csv

```
type,ssize
shirt,xxlarge
shirt,xxlarge
shirt,xlarge
shirt,xlarge
shirt,xlarge
shirt,large
shirt,medium
shirt,small
shirt,small
shirt,xsmall
shirt,xsmall
shirt,xsmall
```

LISTING B.10: shirts.py

```
import pandas as pd

shirts = pd.read_csv("shirts.csv")
print("shirts before:")
print(shirts)
print()

# TECHNIQUE #1:
#shirts.loc[shirts['ssize']=='xxlarge','size'] = 4
#shirts.loc[shirts['ssize']=='xlarge', 'size'] = 4
#shirts.loc[shirts['ssize']=='large',  'size'] = 3
#shirts.loc[shirts['ssize']=='medium', 'size'] = 2
#shirts.loc[shirts['ssize']=='small',  'size'] = 1
#shirts.loc[shirts['ssize']=='xsmall', 'size'] = 1

# TECHNIQUE #2:
#shirts['ssize'].replace('xxlarge', 4, inplace=True)
#shirts['ssize'].replace('xlarge',  4, inplace=True)
#shirts['ssize'].replace('large',   3, inplace=True)
#shirts['ssize'].replace('medium',  2, inplace=True)
#shirts['ssize'].replace('small',   1, inplace=True)
#shirts['ssize'].replace('xsmall',  1, inplace=True)

# TECHNIQUE #3:
#shirts['ssize'] = shirts['ssize'].apply({'xxlarge':4, 'xlarge':4,
'large':3, 'medium':2, 'small':1, 'xsmall':1}.get)
```

```
# TECHNIQUE #4:
shirts['ssize'] = shirts['ssize'].replace(regex='xlarge', value=4)
shirts['ssize'] = shirts['ssize'].replace(regex='large',  value=3)
shirts['ssize'] = shirts['ssize'].replace(regex='medium', value=2)
shirts['ssize'] = shirts['ssize'].replace(regex='small',  value=1)

print("shirts after:")
print(shirts)
```

Listing B.10 starts with a code block of six statements that uses direct comparison with strings to make numeric replacements. For example, the following code snippet replaces all occurrences of the string xxlarge with the value 4:

```
shirts.loc[shirts['ssize']=='xxlarge','size'] = 4
```

The second code block consists of six statements that use the replace() method to perform the same updates, an example of which is shown here:

```
shirts['ssize'].replace('xxlarge', 4, inplace=True)
```

The third code block consists of a single statement that uses the apply() method to perform the same updates, as shown here:

```
shirts['ssize'] = shirts['ssize'].apply({'xxlarge':4, 'xlarge':4,
'large':3, 'medium':2, 'small':1, 'xsmall':1}.get)
```

The fourth code block consists of four statements that use regular expressions to perform the same updates, an example of which is shown here:

```
shirts['ssize'] = shirts['ssize'].replace(regex='xlarge', value=4)
```

Since the preceding code snippet matches xxlarge as well as xlarge, we only need *four* statements instead of six statements. (If you are unfamiliar with regular expressions, you can find the needed information online.) Launch the code in Listing B.10 to see the following output:

```
shirts before
       type    size
0     shirt  xxlarge
1     shirt  xxlarge
2     shirt   xlarge
3     shirt   xlarge
4     shirt   xlarge
5     shirt    large
6     shirt   medium
7     shirt    small
8     shirt    small
9     shirt   xsmall
10    shirt   xsmall
11    shirt   xsmall

shirts after:
       type  size
0     shirt     4
1     shirt     4
```

```
2    shirt    4
3    shirt    4
4    shirt    4
5    shirt    3
6    shirt    2
7    shirt    1
8    shirt    1
9    shirt    1
10   shirt    1
11   shirt    1
```

MATCHING AND SPLITTING STRINGS

Listing B.11 shows the content of `shirts_str.py`, which illustrates how to match a column value with an initial string and how to split a column value based on a letter.

LISTING B.11: shirts_str.py

```python
import pandas as pd

shirts = pd.read_csv("shirts2.csv")
print("shirts:")
print(shirts)
print()

print("shirts starting with xl:")
print(shirts[shirts.ssize.str.startswith('xl')])
print()

print("Exclude 'xlarge' shirts:")
print(shirts[shirts['ssize'] != 'xlarge'])
print()

print("first three letters:")
shirts['sub1'] = shirts['ssize'].str[:3]
print(shirts)
print()

print("split ssize on letter 'a':")
shirts['sub2'] = shirts['ssize'].str.split('a')
print(shirts)
print()

print("Rows 3 through 5 and column 2:")
print(shirts.iloc[2:5, 2])
print()
```

Listing B.11 initializes the data frame `df` with the contents of the CSV file `shirts.csv`, and then displays the contents of `df`. The next code snippet in Listing B.11 uses the `startswith()` method to match the shirt types that start with the letters `xl`, followed by a code snippet that displays the shorts whose size does not equal the string `xlarge`.

The next code snippet uses the construct `str[:3]` to display the first three letters of the shirt types, followed by a code snippet that uses the `split()` method to split the shirt types based on the letter "a."

The final code snippet invokes `iloc[2:5,2]` to display the contents of rows 3 through 5 inclusive, and only the second column. The output of Listing B.11 is as follows:

```
shirts:
      type      ssize
0    shirt    xxlarge
1    shirt    xxlarge
2    shirt     xlarge
3    shirt     xlarge
4    shirt     xlarge
5    shirt      large
6    shirt     medium
7    shirt      small
8    shirt      small
9    shirt     xsmall
10   shirt     xsmall
11   shirt     xsmall

shirts starting with xl:
     type     ssize
2   shirt    xlarge
3   shirt    xlarge
4   shirt    xlarge

Exclude 'xlarge' shirts:
      type      ssize
0    shirt    xxlarge
1    shirt    xxlarge
5    shirt      large
6    shirt     medium
7    shirt      small
8    shirt      small
9    shirt     xsmall
10   shirt     xsmall
11   shirt     xsmall

first three letters:
      type      ssize  sub1
0    shirt    xxlarge   xxl
1    shirt    xxlarge   xxl
2    shirt     xlarge   xla
3    shirt     xlarge   xla
4    shirt     xlarge   xla
5    shirt      large   lar
6    shirt     medium   med
7    shirt      small   sma
8    shirt      small   sma
9    shirt     xsmall   xsm
10   shirt     xsmall   xsm
11   shirt     xsmall   xsm
```

```
split ssize on letter 'a':
      type    ssize sub1        sub2
0    shirt  xxlarge  xxl   [xxl, rge]
1    shirt  xxlarge  xxl   [xxl, rge]
2    shirt   xlarge  xla    [xl, rge]
3    shirt   xlarge  xla    [xl, rge]
4    shirt   xlarge  xla    [xl, rge]
5    shirt    large  lar     [l, rge]
6    shirt   medium  med     [medium]
7    shirt    small  sma     [sm, ll]
8    shirt    small  sma     [sm, ll]
9    shirt   xsmall  xsm    [xsm, ll]
10   shirt   xsmall  xsm    [xsm, ll]
11   shirt   xsmall  xsm    [xsm, ll]

Rows 3 through 5 and column 2:
2    xlarge
3    xlarge
4    xlarge
Name: ssize, dtype: object
```

CONVERTING STRINGS TO DATES

Listing B.12 shows the content of `string2date.py`, which illustrates how to convert strings to date formats.

LISTING B.12: string2date.py

```python
import pandas as pd

bdates1 = {'strdates':  ['20210413','20210813','20211225'],
           'people': ['Sally','Steve','Sarah']
          }

df1 = pd.DataFrame(bdates1, columns = ['strdates','people'])
df1['dates'] = pd.to_datetime(df1['strdates'], format='%Y%m%d')
print("=> Contents of data frame df1:")
print(df1)
print()
print(df1.dtypes)
print()

bdates2 = {'strdates':  ['13Apr2021','08Aug2021','25Dec2021'],
           'people': ['Sally','Steve','Sarah']
          }

df2 = pd.DataFrame(bdates2, columns = ['strdates','people'])
df2['dates'] = pd.to_datetime(df2['strdates'], format='%d%b%Y')
print("=> Contents of data frame df2:")
print(df2)
print()

print(df2.dtypes)
print()
```

Listing B.12 initializes the data frame `df1` with the contents of `bdates1`, and then converts the `strdates` column to dates using the `%Y%m%d` format. The next portion of Listing B.12 initializes the data frame `df2` with the contents of `bdates2`, and then converts the `strdates` column to dates using the `%d%b%Y` format. Launch the code in Listing B.12 to see the following output:

```
=> Contents of data frame df1:
   strdates people       dates
0  20210413  Sally 2021-04-13
1  20210813  Steve 2021-08-13
2  20211225  Sarah 2021-12-25


strdates              object
people                object
dates         datetime64[ns]
dtype: object


=> Contents of data frame df2:
    strdates people       dates
0  13Apr2021  Sally 2021-04-13
1  08Aug2021  Steve 2021-08-08
2  25Dec2021  Sarah 2021-12-25


strdates              object
people                object
dates         datetime64[ns]
dtype: object
```

WORKING WITH DATE RANGES

Listing B.13 shows the content of `pand_parse_dates.py` that illustrates how to work with date ranges in a CSV file.

LISTING B.13: pand_parse_dates.py

```python
import pandas as pd

df = pd.read_csv('multiple_dates.csv', parse_dates=['dates'])

print("df:")
print(df)
print()


df = df.set_index(['dates'])
start_d = "2021-04-30"
end_d   = "2021-08-31"

print("DATES BETWEEN",start_d,"AND",end_d,":")
print(df.loc[start_d:end_d])
print()


print("DATES BEFORE",start_d,":")
print(df.loc[df.index < start_d])
```

```
years = ['2020','2021','2022']
for year in years:
  year_sum = df.loc[year].sum()[0]
  print("SUM OF VALUES FOR YEAR",year,":",year_sum)
```

Listing B.13 starts by initializing the variable df with the contents of the CSV file multiple_dates.csv and then displaying its contents. The next code snippet sets the dates column as the index column and then initializes the variable start_d and end_d that contain a start date and an end date, respectively.

The next portion of Listing B.13 displays the dates between start_d and end_d, and then the list of dates that precede start_d. The final code block iterates through a list of years and then calculates the sum of the numbers in the values field for each year in the list. Launch the code in Listing B.13 to see the following output:

```
df:
          dates  values
0   2020-01-31    40.0
1   2020-02-28    45.0
2   2020-03-31    56.0
3   2021-04-30     NaN
4   2021-05-31     NaN
5   2021-06-30   140.0
6   2021-07-31    95.0
7   2022-08-31    40.0
8   2022-09-30    55.0
9   2022-10-31     NaN
10  2022-11-15    65.0

DATES BETWEEN 2021-04-30 AND 2021-08-31 :
            values
dates
2021-04-30     NaN
2021-05-31     NaN
2021-06-30   140.0
2021-07-31    95.0

DATES BEFORE 2021-04-30 :
            values
dates
2020-01-31    40.0
2020-02-28    45.0
2020-03-31    56.0

SUM OF VALUES FOR YEAR 2020 : 141.0
SUM OF VALUES FOR YEAR 2021 : 235.0
SUM OF VALUES FOR YEAR 2022 : 160.0
```

DETECTING MISSING DATES

Listing B.14 shows the content of pandas_missing_dates.py that illustrates how to detect missing date values in a CSV file.

LISTING B.14: pandas_missing_dates.py

```python
import pandas as pd

# A data frame from a dictionary of lists
data = {'Date': ['2021-01-18', '2021-01-20', '2021-01-21', '2021-01-24'],
        'Name': ['Joe', 'John', 'Jane', 'Jim']}
df = pd.DataFrame(data)

# Setting the Date values as index:
df = df.set_index('Date')

# to_datetime() converts string format to a DateTime object:
df.index = pd.to_datetime(df.index)

start_d="2021-01-18"
end_d="2021-01-25"

# display dates that are not in the sequence:
print("MISSING DATES BETWEEN",start_d,"and",end_d,":")
dates = pd.date_range(start=start_d, end=end_d).difference(df.index)

for date in dates:
  print("date:",date)
print()
```

Listing B.14 initializes the dictionary `data` with a list of values for the `Date` field and the `Name` field, after which the variable `df` is initialized as a data frame whose contents are from the `data` variable.

The next code snippet sets the `Date` field as the index of the data frame `df`, after which the string-based dates are converted to `DateTime` objects. Another pair of code snippets initialize the variable `start_d` and `end_d` with a start date and an end date, respectively.

The final portion of Listing B.14 initializes the variable `dates` with the list of missing dates between `start_d` and `end_d`, after which the contents of `dates` are displayed. Launch the code in Listing B.14 to see the following output:

```
MISSING DATES BETWEEN 2021-01-18 and 2021-01-25 :
date: 2022-01-19 00:00:00
date: 2022-01-22 00:00:00
date: 2022-01-23 00:00:00
date: 2022-01-25 00:00:00
```

INTERPOLATING MISSING DATES

Listing B.15 shows the content of `missing_dates.csv` and Listing B.16 shows the content of `pandas_interpolate.py` that illustrate how to replace `NaN` values with interpolated values that are calculated in several ways.

LISTING B.15: missing_dates.csv

```
"dates","values"
2021-01-31,40
2021-02-28,45
2021-03-31,56
2021-04-30,NaN
2021-05-31,NaN
2021-06-30,140
2021-07-31,95
2021-08-31,40
2021-09-30,55
2021-10-31,NaN
2021-11-15,65
```

Notice the value 140 (shown in bold) in Listing B.15: this value is an outlier, which will affect the calculation of the interpolated values, and potentially generate additional outliers.

LISTING B.16: pandas_interpolate.py

```
import pandas as pd
df = pd.read_csv("missing_dates.csv")

# fill NaN values with linear interpolation:
df1 = df.interpolate()

# fill NaN values with quadratic polynomial interpolation:
df2 = df.interpolate(method='polynomial', order=2)

# fill NaN values with cubic polynomial interpolation:
df3 = df.interpolate(method='polynomial', order=3)

print("original data frame:")
print(df)
print()
print("linear interpolation:")
print(df1)
print()
print("quadratic interpolation:")
print(df2)
print()
print("cubic interpolation:")
print(df3)
print()
```

Listing B.16 initializes df with the contents of the CSV file missing_dates.csv and then initializes the three data frames df1, df2, and df3 that are based on linear, quadratic, and cubic interpolation, respectively, via the interpolate() method. Launch the code in Listing B.16 to see the following output:

```
original data frame:
        dates  values
0   2021-01-31    40.0
```

```
1    2021-02-28     45.0
2    2021-03-31     56.0
3    2021-04-30      NaN
4    2021-05-31      NaN
5    2021-06-30    140.0
6    2021-07-31     95.0
7    2021-08-31     40.0
8    2021-09-30     55.0
9    2021-10-31      NaN
10   2021-11-15     65.0


linear interpolation:
        dates  values
0    2021-01-31     40.0
1    2021-02-28     45.0
2    2021-03-31     56.0
3    2021-04-30     84.0
4    2021-05-31    112.0
5    2021-06-30    140.0
6    2021-07-31     95.0
7    2021-08-31     40.0
8    2021-09-30     55.0
9    2021-10-31     60.0
10   2021-11-15     65.0


quadratic interpolation:
        dates      values
0    2021-01-31     40.000000
1    2021-02-28     45.000000
2    2021-03-31     56.000000
3    2021-04-30     88.682998
4    2021-05-31    136.002883
5    2021-06-30    140.000000
6    2021-07-31     95.000000
7    2021-08-31     40.000000
8    2021-09-30     55.000000
9    2021-10-31     68.162292
10   2021-11-15     65.000000


cubic interpolation:
        dates      values
0    2021-01-31     40.000000
1    2021-02-28     45.000000
2    2021-03-31     56.000000
3    2021-04-30     92.748096
4    2021-05-31    132.055687
5    2021-06-30    140.000000
6    2021-07-31     95.000000
7    2021-08-31     40.000000
8    2021-09-30     55.000000
9    2021-10-31     91.479905
10   2021-11-15     65.000000
```

OTHER OPERATIONS WITH DATES

Listing B.17 shows the content of `pandas_misc1.py` that illustrates how to extract a list of years from a column in a data frame.

LISTING B.17: pandas_misc1.py

```
import pandas as pd
import numpy as np

df = pd.read_csv('multiple_dates.csv', parse_dates=['dates'])
print("df:")
print(df)
print()

year_list = df['dates']

arr1 = np.array([])
for long_year in year_list:
  year = str(long_year)
  short_year = year[0:4]
  arr1 = np.append(arr1,short_year)

unique_years = set(arr1)
print("unique_years:")
print(unique_years)
print()

unique_arr = np.array(pd.Data frame.from_dict(unique_years))
print("unique_arr:")
print(unique_arr)
print()
```

Listing B.17 initializes `df` with the contents of the CSV file `multiple_dates.csv` and then displays its contents. The next portion of Listing B.17 initializes `year_list` with the dates column of `df`.

The next code block contains a loop that iterates through the elements in `year_list`, extracts the first four characters (i.e., the year value) and appends that substring to the NumPy array `arr1`. The final code block initializes the variable `unique_arr` as a NumPy array consisting of the unique years in the dictionary `unique_years`. Launch the code in Listing B.17 to see the following output:

```
df:
        dates  values
0  2020-01-31    40.0
1  2020-02-28    45.0
2  2020-03-31    56.0
3  2021-04-30     NaN
4  2021-05-31     NaN
5  2021-06-30   140.0
6  2021-07-31    95.0
```

```
7   2022-08-31      40.0
8   2022-09-30      55.0
9   2022-10-31      NaN
10  2022-11-15      65.0

unique_years:
{'2022', '2020', '2021'}

unique_arr:
[['2022']
 ['2020']
 ['2021']]
```

Listing B.18 shows the content of `pandas_misc2.py` that illustrates how to iterate through the rows of a data frame. Row-wise iteration is not recommended because it can result in performance issues in larger datasets.

LISTING B.18: pandas_misc2.py

```python
import pandas as pd

df = pd.read_csv('multiple_dates.csv', parse_dates=['dates'])

print("df:")
print(df)
print()

print("=> ITERATE THROUGH THE ROWS:")
for idx,row in df.iterrows():
  print("idx:",idx," year:",row['dates'])
print()
```

Listing B.18 initializes the data frame `df`, prints its contents, and then processes the rows of `df` in a loop. During each iteration, the current index and row contents are displayed. Launch the code in Listing B.18 to see the following output:

```
df:
        dates    values
0   2020-01-31     40.0
1   2020-02-28     45.0
2   2020-03-31     56.0
3   2021-04-30     NaN
4   2021-05-31     NaN
5   2021-06-30    140.0
6   2021-07-31     95.0
7   2022-08-31     40.0
8   2022-09-30     55.0
9   2022-10-31     NaN
10  2022-11-15     65.0

=> ITERATE THROUGH THE ROWS:
idx: 0  year: 2020-01-31 00:00:00
idx: 1  year: 2020-02-28 00:00:00
```

```
idx: 2   year: 2020-03-31 00:00:00
idx: 3   year: 2021-04-30 00:00:00
idx: 4   year: 2021-05-31 00:00:00
idx: 5   year: 2021-06-30 00:00:00
idx: 6   year: 2021-07-31 00:00:00
idx: 7   year: 2022-08-31 00:00:00
idx: 8   year: 2022-09-30 00:00:00
idx: 9   year: 2022-10-31 00:00:00
idx: 10  year: 2022-11-15 00:00:00
```

Listing B.19 shows the content of `pandas_misc3.py` that illustrates how to display a weekly set of dates that are between a start date and an end date.

LISTING B.19: pandas_misc3.py

```
import pandas as pd

start_d="01/02/2022"
end_d="12/02/2022"
weekly_dates=pd.date_range(start=start_d, end=end_d, freq='W')

print("Weekly dates from",start_d,"to",end_d,":")
print(weekly_dates)
```

Listing B.19 starts with initializing the variable `start_d` and `end_d` that contain a start date and an end date, respectively, and then initializes the variable `weekly_dates` with a list of weekly dates between the start date and the end date. Launch the code in Listing B.19 to see the following output:

```
Weekly dates from 01/02/2022 to 12/02/2022 :
DatetimeIndex(['2022-01-02', '2022-01-09', '2022-01-16', '2022-01-23',
               '2022-01-30', '2022-02-06', '2022-02-13', '2022-02-20',
               '2022-02-27', '2022-03-06', '2022-03-13', '2022-03-20',
               '2022-03-27', '2022-04-03', '2022-04-10', '2022-04-17',
               '2022-04-24', '2022-05-01', '2022-05-08', '2022-05-15',
               '2022-05-22', '2022-05-29', '2022-06-05', '2022-06-12',
               '2022-06-19', '2022-06-26', '2022-07-03', '2022-07-10',
               '2022-07-17', '2022-07-24', '2022-07-31', '2022-08-07',
               '2022-08-14', '2022-08-21', '2022-08-28', '2022-09-04',
               '2022-09-11', '2022-09-18', '2022-09-25', '2022-10-02',
               '2022-10-09', '2022-10-16', '2022-10-23', '2022-10-30',
               '2022-11-06', '2022-11-13', '2022-11-20', '2022-11-27'],
              dtype='datetime64[ns]', freq='W-SUN')
```

MERGING AND SPLITTING COLUMNS

Listing B.20 shows the content of `employees.csv` and Listing B.21 shows the content of `emp_merge_split.py`. These examples illustrate how to merge columns and split columns of a CSV file.

LISTING B.20: employees.csv

```
name,year,month
Jane-Smith,2015,Aug
Dave-Smith,2020,Jan
Jane-Jones,2018,Dec
Jane-Stone,2017,Feb
Dave-Stone,2014,Apr
Mark-Aster,,Oct
Jane-Jones,NaN,Jun
```

LISTING B.21: emp_merge_split.py

```python
import pandas as pd

emps = pd.read_csv("employees.csv")
print("emps:")
print(emps)
print()

emps['year']  = emps['year'].astype(str)
emps['month'] = emps['month'].astype(str)

# separate column for first name and for last name:
emps['fname'],emps['lname'] = emps['name'].str.split("-",1).str

# concatenate year and month with a "#" symbol:
emps['hdate1'] = emps['year'].astype(str)+"#"+emps['month'].astype(str)

# concatenate year and month with a "-" symbol:
emps['hdate2'] = emps[['year','month']].agg('-'.join, axis=1)

print(emps)
print()
```

Listing B.21 initializes the data frame `df` with the contents of the CSV file `employees.csv`, and then displays the contents of `df`. The next pair of code snippets invoke the `astype()` method to convert the contents of the `year` and `month` columns to strings.

The next code snippet in Listing B.21 uses the `split()` method to split the `name` column into the columns `fname` and `lname` that contain the first name and last name, respectively, of each employee's name:

```python
emps['fname'],emps['lname'] = emps['name'].str.split("-",1).str
```

The next code snippet concatenates the contents of the year and month string with a "#" character to create a new column called `hdate1`:

```python
emps['hdate1'] = emps['year'].astype(str)+"#"+emps['month'].astype(str)
```

The final code snippet concatenates the contents of the `year` and `month` string with a "-" to create a new column called `hdate2`, as shown here:

```python
emps['hdate2'] = emps[['year','month']].agg('-'.join, axis=1)
```

Launch the code in Listing B.21 to see the following output:

```
emps:
        name      year month
0   Jane-Smith  2015.0   Aug
1   Dave-Smith  2020.0   Jan
2   Jane-Jones  2018.0   Dec
3   Jane-Stone  2017.0   Feb
4   Dave-Stone  2014.0   Apr
5   Mark-Aster     NaN   Oct
6   Jane-Jones     NaN   Jun

        name      year month fname  lname      hdate1       hdate2
0   Jane-Smith  2015.0   Aug  Jane  Smith  2015.0#Aug  2015.0-Aug
1   Dave-Smith  2020.0   Jan  Dave  Smith  2020.0#Jan  2020.0-Jan
2   Jane-Jones  2018.0   Dec  Jane  Jones  2018.0#Dec  2018.0-Dec
3   Jane-Stone  2017.0   Feb  Jane  Stone  2017.0#Feb  2017.0-Feb
4   Dave-Stone  2014.0   Apr  Dave  Stone  2014.0#Apr  2014.0-Apr
5   Mark-Aster     nan   Oct  Mark  Aster     nan#Oct     nan-Oct
6   Jane-Jones     nan   Jun  Jane  Jones     nan#Jun     nan-Jun
```

There is one other detail regarding the following commented-out code snippet:

```
#emps['fname'],emps['lname'] = emps['name'].str.split("-",1).str
```

The following deprecation message is displayed if you uncomment the preceding code snippet:

```
#FutureWarning: Columnar iteration over characters
#will be deprecated in future releases.
```

READING HTML WEB PAGES

Listing B.22 displays the contents of the HTML Web page `abc.html`. Listing B.23 shows the content of `read_html_page.py` that illustrates how to read the contents of an HTML Web page from Pandas. Note that this code will only work with Web pages that contain *at least* one HTML `<table>` element.

LISTING B.22: abc.html

```
<html>
<head>
</head>
<body>
  <table>
    <tr>
      <td>hello from abc.html!</td>
    </tr>
  </table>
</body>
</html>
```

LISTING B.23: read_html_page.py

```
import pandas as pd

file_name="abc.html"
with open(file_name, "r") as f:
  dfs = pd.read_html(f.read())

print("Contents of HTML Table(s) in the HTML Web Page:")
print(dfs)
```

Listing B.23 starts with an `import` statement, followed by initializing the variable `file_name` to `abc.html` that is displayed in Listing B.22. The next code snippet initializes the variable `dfs` as a data frame with the contents of the HTML Web page `abc.html`. The final portion of Listing B.19 displays the contents of the data frame `dsf`. Launch the code in Listing B.23 to see the following output:

```
Contents of HTML Table(s) in the HTML Web Page:
[                          0
0  hello from abc.html!]
```

For more information about the `read_html()` method, navigate to this URL:

https://pandas.pydata.org/pandas-docs/stable/reference/api/

SAVING A DATA FRAME AS AN HTML WEB PAGE

Listing B.24 shows the content of `read_html_page.py` that illustrates how to read the contents of an HTML Web page from Pandas. Note that this code will only work with Web pages that contain at least one HTML `<table>` element.

LISTING B.24: read_html_page.py

```
import pandas as pd

emps = pd.read_csv("employees.csv")
print("emps:")
print(emps)
print()

emps['year']  = emps['year'].astype(str)
emps['month'] = emps['month'].astype(str)

# separate column for first name and for last name:
emps['fname'],emps['lname'] = emps['name'].str.split("-",1).str

# concatenate year and month with a "#" symbol:
emps['hdate1'] = emps['year'].astype(str)+"#"+emps['month'].astype(str)

# concatenate year and month with a "-" symbol:
emps['hdate2'] = emps[['year','month']].agg('-'.join, axis=1)
```

```
print(emps)
print()

html = emps.to_html()
print("Data frame as an HTML Web Page:")
print(html)
```

Listing B.24 populates the data frame `temps` with the contents of `employees.csv`, and then converts the `year` and `month` attributes to type string. The next code snippet splits the contents of the `name` field with the "-" symbol as a delimiter. As a result, this code snippet populates the new `fname` and `lname` fields with the first name and last name, respectively, of the previously split field.

The next code snippet in Listing B.24 converts the `year` and `month` fields to strings, and then concatenates them with a "#" as a delimiter. Yet another code snippet populates the `hdate2` field with the concatenation of the year and month fields.

After displaying the content of the data frame `emps`, the final code snippet populates the variable `html` with the result of converting the data frame `emps` to an HTML Web page by invoking the `to_html()` method of Pandas. Launch the code in Listing B.24 to see the following output:

```
Contents of HTML Table(s)
emps:
         name      year month
0   Jane-Smith  2015.0    Aug
1   Dave-Smith  2020.0    Jan
2   Jane-Jones  2018.0    Dec
3   Jane-Stone  2017.0    Feb
4   Dave-Stone  2014.0    Apr
5   Mark-Aster     NaN    Oct
6   Jane-Jones     NaN    Jun


         name      year month fname  lname       hdate1       hdate2
0   Jane-Smith  2015.0    Aug  Jane  Smith  2015.0#Aug  2015.0-Aug
1   Dave-Smith  2020.0    Jan  Dave  Smith  2020.0#Jan  2020.0-Jan
2   Jane-Jones  2018.0    Dec  Jane  Jones  2018.0#Dec  2018.0-Dec
3   Jane-Stone  2017.0    Feb  Jane  Stone  2017.0#Feb  2017.0-Feb
4   Dave-Stone  2014.0    Apr  Dave  Stone  2014.0#Apr  2014.0-Apr
5   Mark-Aster     nan    Oct  Mark  Aster    nan#Oct     nan-Oct
6   Jane-Jones     nan    Jun  Jane  Jones    nan#Jun     nan-Jun

Data frame as an HTML Web Page:
<table border="1" class="data frame">
  <thead>
    <tr style="text-align: right;">
      <th></th>
      <th>name</th>
      <th>year</th>
      <th>month</th>
      <th>fname</th>
      <th>lname</th>
      <th>hdate1</th>
      <th>hdate2</th>
    </tr>
  </thead>
```

```
<tbody>
  <tr>
    <th>0</th>
    <td>Jane-Smith</td>
    <td>2015.0</td>
    <td>Aug</td>
    <td>Jane</td>
    <td>Smith</td>
    <td>2015.0#Aug</td>
    <td>2015.0-Aug</td>
  </tr>
  <tr>
    <th>1</th>
    <td>Dave-Smith</td>
    <td>2020.0</td>
    <td>Jan</td>
    <td>Dave</td>
    <td>Smith</td>
    <td>2020.0#Jan</td>
    <td>2020.0-Jan</td>
  </tr>
  // details omitted for brevity
  <tr>
    <th>6</th>
    <td>Jane-Jones</td>
    <td>nan</td>
    <td>Jun</td>
    <td>Jane</td>
    <td>Jones</td>
    <td>nan#Jun</td>
    <td>nan-Jun</td>
  </tr>
</tbody>
</table>
```

SUMMARY

This appendix introduced you to Pandas for creating labeled data frames and displaying the metadata of data frames. Then, you learned how to create data frames from various sources of data, such as random numbers and hard-coded data values. In addition, you saw how to perform column-based and row-based operations in Pandas data frames.

You also learned how to create a Pandas data frame from a NumPy array, as well as how to create Pandas data frames from data stored in CSV files.

INDEX

www.ingramcontent.com/pod-product-compliance
Lightning Source LLC
LaVergne TN
LVHW062315060326
832902LV00013B/2233